# THE BIG PICTURE

## MAKING GOD THE MAIN FOCUS OF YOUR LIFE

HAYLEY & MICHAEL DiMARCO

B&H
PUBLISHING GROUP

Nashville, Tennessee

Copyright © 2013 by B&H Publishing Group
All rights reserved. Printed in the United States of America.
978-1-4336-7972-8
Published by B&H Publishing Group
Nashville, Tennessee

Dewey Decimal Classification: 248.834
Subject Heading: GOD / TEENAGERS / GOSPEL

1 2 3 4 5 6 7    17 16 15 14 13

# CONTENTS

# INTRODUCTION

> You alone are Yahweh. You created the heavens, the highest heavens with all their host, the earth and all that is on it, the seas and all that is in them. You give life to all of them, and the heavenly host worships You.
> (Nehemiah 9:6)

## FOCUS!

When you look at the world around you, you focus on the most important stuff. It might be the stuff you love, or it might be the stuff you hate. Some people focus on their trials, while others focus on their successes. Are you a glass-half-full or a glass-half-empty person? What do you think about the most?

### What's the focus of your life?

How you answer these questions will determine not only your today, your tomorrow, and your future, but will affect your emotional and spiritual life as well. The focus of your life is your magnetic North; everything you do toward that focus becomes the highest priority in your life.

If the main priority in your life is to stop the pain, then your focus might be whatever you can do to medicate that pain. If the center of your life is someone you love, then you will do whatever you can to keep that person in your life. But no matter what your focus, there is a lot going on around it, a lot you can't ignore, a lot that's meant for you. And as long as your focus is on the **stuff** of this world, then you're missing the most important thing. You're missing the big picture. Seeing the big picture, instead of wasting energy on one or two things that ultimately don't matter, is the most freeing and powerful action you could ever take.

It can be easy to see yourself as the focus of your life. We all start out that way. You hear your own thoughts, feel your own feelings, do stuff to and with yourself more than anyone else in the world, but that doesn't make you the star. See, when you're the star of your own life, when it's all about you and your happiness, your comfort, and your success, then life is a real roller coaster. There are dangers all around you: dangers to your life, happiness, comfort, and success, which you are ultimately powerless to change. When you focus on yourself and bad things happen, the first thing to suffer is your self-esteem. And that's because your self-life has suffered, so the roller coaster takes a dive and all the bad feelings pile on. Self-esteem—the stuff that looks inside and determines the value and the beauty of life based on self—is volatile, threatening to blow up at any second. And that's why self-esteem and all the work that goes into raising it is in vain. No matter how much success you find, you will never be the real focus of this world, so your self-esteem will never be totally maintained. But that's just one reason why self-esteem is an immaterial thing. Instead, there is something essential, something that is the ultimate source of peace, joy, and true success, and that something is God-esteem.

**When your life isn't dependent on your success but His, then your life is the definition of successful.**

No matter what happens to you or in you or around you, you are a pure success because your esteem is found in the one who is totally perfect, totally powerful, and totally divine.

Esteem involves the idea of vision, of looking at something. And as long as you are looking at yourself and thinking that you are the big picture, then you will see only a teeny tiny part of the whole. But when you stop looking in the mirror and start looking at the bigger picture of a life made for more than your success or failure, you will find all the goodness and hope that you have ever desired. In fact, rather than seeing the glass half full you will see it overflowing!

You weren't meant to live with nothing but your little world in focus. You were meant to see the

**to grasp the depth of God's love for you and all of creation**. To see His hand on every moment of your life. To see His glory in every event in history, and to see His power in every moment of your past, present, and future life. If you can't look around you and say, "I see God in that," then your life isn't free. You are in chains to the world. But if you are ready to be set free, if you want to walk away from the doubt, the fear, the worry, the drama, then stand back and look at the *Big Picture*. Making God the focus, the priority, the center of your world, with all its suffering and success, will give meaning to every moment and make it all part of an amazing story of true love that can never be matched.

The amazing thing is that **God has been with us**

**from the very beginning**, He is with us today and will never leave us. As you step back and start to get a bigger perspective on our planet, as you start to see God as actively involved and working in your life you will see that nothing is left to chance. You will start to understand the reason why you exist, and you will begin to take hold of the plans He has for you, to prosper you and not to harm you, to give you hope and a future. Knowing the history of the world, seeing the big picture and your role in it is bound to change your life today and forevermore. So let's dive into the big picture and see the God whose story explains it all.

# CHAPTER 1
# GOD WITH YOU

> *God's dwelling is with humanity, and He will live with them. They will be His people, and God Himself will be with them and be their God.* (Revelation 21:3)

If you could create an artificial life form, would you do it? If you knew that it would be your best friend, that it would be your constant companion, that it would look like you, act like you, serve you, love you, would you build it? What if you knew that all that would happen but one day it would attack you? That one day it would not only attack you viciously, but that it would hurt you so badly that you would die. Would you do it? Would you still create it for all the good times, knowing that the bad times would come all too soon?

Chances are your answer would be no. Creating something that will one day kill you doesn't sound like a good idea, does it? But that's exactly what God did when He created man. He made a creature that would one day reject Him, accuse Him, and want to kill Him. It might sound crazy, but it's true. **When God created the world He knew how it would all play out.** He didn't make the earth, the water, the sky, the plants, the animals, and man, then sit back in wonder to see what would happen next. Nope, **God is omniscient.** That means He knows it all. He knows the past, the present, and the future. So that means that at the moment God said "Let there be light," He was creating the very planet that He knew He would one day send His Son into, so that He might die a horrible death at the hand of His own creation. Knowing this about Him is the first step to making Him the focus of your life. Without knowing His omniscience you can't fully appreciate or understand His love or His kindness. But knowing this stimulates the brain to ask the question "Why?" Why would He do it?

**Why would God, knowing full well the story of mankind and our sinful choices, create us at all?**

The answer to that question will tell you a lot about the Creator and His creation.

# GOD WITH US AT THE BEGINNING

In order to answer the question "Why?" we have to step back and take a look at the big picture from the beginning. And we get a glimpse into the beginning in the Gospel of John. Take a look:

> In the beginning was the Word, and the Word was with God, and the Word was God. He was with God in the beginning. All things were created through Him, and apart from Him not one thing was created that has been created. Life was in Him, and that life was the light of men. That light shines in the darkness, yet the darkness did not overcome it. (John 1:1–5)

"In the beginning," we read, "was the Word." So before there was earth or sky, water or land, plant or animal, there was this Word. But what or who is the Word you ask? And that's a good question. If you've been in church much, you might have heard that the Word is Jesus. And that would be correct. But there's so much more to this statement than just being told, "Hey, just replace 'Word' with 'Jesus.'" Understanding that God didn't just randomly call Jesus the Word explains something about His very nature that matters to your life, because

# what you think about God is the single most important thing about you.

And if you don't allow your thoughts about God to go deeper than "that's just what someone told me," then you haven't discovered the depths that God wants to take you in relationship to Him. And that's the point of *The Big Picture*, we want you to realize that the Bible, often called the *Word* of God, is the story of God and His desire for a relationship with you. If you want more God in your life, and so more of the stuff He fills the life of faith with—stuff like peace, hope, joy, patience and so much more—then dive into the story of God and find out who He is and why He chose to create us at all.

So let's dive back into the Word and find out more about the God whose story you are a part of. So "**the Word" is another name for Jesus**, but why did God call Him the Word? Well, first of all, you can't take it literally. That probably goes without saying, but Jesus isn't literally the word $w$-$o$-$r$-$d$. God is using a metaphor, like He does a lot of times in the Bible. A metaphor is used to explain something that is real, by comparing it to something that people easily understand. Like when Jesus says, "I am the door," in John 10:9, He doesn't mean He's made out of wood with a door handle for a belly button. Jesus isn't actually a wooden door, but spiritually speaking He is the door that leads to a life with God, the door that protects us from intruders and keeps us safe. So the metaphor of a door makes a lot of sense to the human mind that sees doors all day long and understands their function. So like "door," **"Word" also had a meaning that the Greeks of John's time would have understood *as the nature of the cosmos, or rational thought or speech.*** So when the early readers of the Bible saw *logos*, Greek for *word*, they would have understood its deeper meaning. It made Word with a capital W easily understood as God Himself, the Creator of the cosmos and the Source of all rational thought and speech.

So **the Word is God Himself**, but Jesus, not God the Father. How do we know that? Because in verse 1 the first thing it says isn't that "the Word was God," but "that the Word was *with* God." In other words, God wasn't alone. After it establishes this relationship, Scripture goes on to say that "the Word was God." He was with God and He was God. Now this idea can throw any sane mind for a loop. How can He *be* Him and *be with* Him at the same time? How can the two become one? A good way to understand this is by thinking about a husband and a wife. They are two people, but when they marry they become one (see Genesis 2:24). In a similar way,

## God, Jesus, and the Holy Spirit are three, but they are also one.

They live in community, and it was in this community that they formed the world. The third person of this community you can read about in Genesis 1:1–2, *"In the beginning God created the heavens and the earth. Now the earth was formless and empty, darkness covered the surface of the watery depths, and the **Spirit of God** was hovering over the surface of the waters."* So, in the beginning, we have God the Father, God the Son, and God the Holy Spirit. This relational nature of God, three in one, is referred to as the Trinity, and it plays an important role in understanding your relationship with God. More on this later.

Next, you can see in verse 3 that *"all things were created through Him and apart from Him not one thing was created*." Did you know that? Did you know that **the Son of God didn't just come into being at the time He became a man, but that He was there at creation**? Not only was He there for creation but He is responsible for the creation. You can know that because of what comes next: "*apart from Him not one thing was created that has been created*" (v. 3b). Colossians 1:15–20 says the same kind of thing when talking about Jesus, "*He is the image of the invisible God, the firstborn over all creation. For everything was created by Him, in heaven and on earth, the visible and the invisible, whether thrones or dominions or rulers or authorities—all things have been created through Him and for Him.*" So, if all things were created through Him, that means there is nothing that wasn't created by Him. In other words, there is nothing before Him. This speaks to a very important thing about God that you need to wrap your brain around and that is that **God is self-existent**. No one created Him. He has always been. Like it says in John 5:26, He "*has life in Himself.*" Now, after reading Colossians 1:15 you might be screaming, "But it says that He was the 'firstborn.' Doesn't that mean He was created, born?" It sure sounds like it, but you have to understand the language of the Bible. See, "firstborn" is used numerous times in the Old Testament to describe someone who is supreme or has a special place in God the Father's heart. For example Israel is referred to as God's firstborn son, but that doesn't mean God doesn't love other nations. So, in the same way, the term describes The son's supremacy, His place in God's heart, and not His being born or made by anything or anyone.

The idea of self-existence is inconceivable to the human mind that knows nothing of anything that wasn't first created. The closest you can probably come to the concept is to remember your childhood, when you felt like your parents had always existed. When you were a wee one, you had no concept of your parents having ever been born or having lived a childhood like yours, but as you found out as you grew, they too were the result of their parents' union. But,

**in order for God to be God He cannot have a cause beside Himself.**

The fact that God has no parents, no creator, no one who caused Him to come into being, shows the difference between Him and all the rest of creation—creation has a cause, and that's God. So **everything was made by someone who was made by no one**. Wow, mind blowing, huh? This is what makes Him God. If He were created, then wouldn't it be His creator that would be the real God?

If this idea makes you uncomfortable because you can't wrap your brain around it, you're not alone. People have struggled with this stuff for eons. But if you look for answers in Scripture, you will see that God confirms this one leap of faith when He says, "*No god was formed before Me, and there will be none after Me. I, I am Yahweh, and there is no other Savior but Me*" (Isaiah 43:10–11). The self-existence of God is foundational to Him being God and to your not being God.

Now back to our verse. Verse 4 tells us that, "*Life was in Him, and that life was the light of men.*" You have to know here that we are not talking about the life of Jesus on the earth, but at the time of creation. It's the same Person, and He is still referred to as the *light of men*. And that is important to the story of creation because it was His life that gave us light, as in "*let there be light*" (Genesis 1:3). And the light that reveals the glory of God—in other words, the beauty of God here on the earth—points us back to Him. It shows us the difference between bad and good, evil and righteousness, and helps us to see God in our world. Romans 1 confirms that the creation is a light that points back to God: "*For His invisible attributes, that is, His eternal power and divine nature, have been clearly seen since the creation of the world, being understood through what He has made*" (Romans 1:20). The light of men, the Word, shines bright enough for us to see His eternal power and His divine nature in His creation. This light, that is so evident in the world, points us back to heaven and to the life of the Creator Himself.

# So the creation story teaches the eternity of God. He is infinite, He goes on and on in all directions.

His being knows no beginning and no end. Like most of the attributes of God, His infiniteness is incomprehensible to humans. This is just another thing unique to God. If God were comprehensible by man, that would mean man could fathom Him in totality and, so, limit Him. But the very nature of His infiniteness means He cannot be limited, can't be measured, and so can't be fully understood. He is, after all, God! That word has lost some of its power through overuse, but its true meaning points directly at His infiniteness. To help you get this concept, let's give you a word picture. C. S. Lewis once compared the endlessness of God to a long piece of paper that goes on to infinity in either direction, and time, or the beginning of it, as a small line on the paper that extends only a short distance. God goes on forever in both directions, while man is finite and only exists in a small section of the paper. With this thought in mind, you can also kind of get a picture of His **omnipresence.** Since **He lives beyond measure, He also lives beyond the measure of time, and so time and space don't constrain Him.** That means He can effortlessly be all places at all times. His presence, like all of His other attributes, is limitless and infinite. And that's essential to any understanding of God. **Everything about Him is limitless, He doesn't run out of anything or need anything or anyone because He has all He needs; He is completely self-sufficient** (see Psalm 50:12). This infinite nature of God should be in the front of your mind in any discussion of His nature, so keep hold of this idea and let it stew in your brain, so it will season all of your other thoughts on God.

# GOD WITH US IN RELATIONSHIP

So why did God create, if it wasn't out of need? Why did He create the world at all, when He knew what pain it would bring Him? You might ask a woman the same question about her desire to have a baby. Childbirth can be hours and hours of agony. And raising a baby takes every ounce of energy and strength from the mother. For her child, she has to deny herself sleep and a lot of her own desires. For her child, she gives the best of herself. And why does she do it? Because of the love that overflows out of her to this baby, who is part of herself.

**God didn't create man because He was lonely; He was not alone, He lived in community.**

And that's important, because it tells you that God is relational. He isn't an island. He isn't an isolated being that exists in solitude, but a being that exists in a community of three. **He is a God of relationship.** A lot of people talk about God as if He's distant, far removed from His creation. Some think He just made the world and then walked away from it. What an idea! Thinking that God is absent, that He is hands-off or gone completely, is inconsistent with who the Bible says He is. And it makes no sense, when you think about it, because **God's purpose in creating was to share Himself with His creation.** After all, He didn't need the creation to meet any kind of need because, in His self-existent and endlessness, He has all He needs for eternity. He wasn't lacking something that making people would fix for Him. But He was so filled with love and goodness that He wanted to share it, and so He created. Like parents who want a child to share their love with, so the Trinity created the world to share themselves with us.

**What did God want to share** exactly? There is one overarching thing that describes best what God wanted to reveal to humanity, and that is His glory. **His glory is the display of His nature.** His love, mercy, grace, goodness, kindness, wrath, justice, beauty, patience, majesty, power, and the list goes on, is all part of His glory. Just take a look at the beauty of the Grand Canyon or the perfection of a bubbling brook running through a majestic forest, and you can sense the glory of God being shown to you. Then think of the deep sense of relief, or of the goose bumps that run across your skin, or even of the joy that you can get just from looking at God's creation. This is a visual example of how God displays His glory to you. And that's exactly what He did when He created; He opened Himself up to His creation. To create the world and then to walk away from it isn't to share yourself fully. And that's not what God did; in fact, nothing could be further from the truth. God created so that He could live with His creation, and share all of Himself with it.

And so on the sixth day He said, *"'Let Us make man in Our image, according to Our likeness. They will rule the fish of the sea, the birds of the sky, the livestock, all the earth, and the creatures that crawl on the earth.'*

*So God created man in His own image; He created him in the image of God; He created them male and female. God blessed them, and God said to them, 'Be fruitful, multiply, fill the earth, and subdue it. Rule the fish of the sea, the birds of the sky, and every creature that crawls on the earth'"* (Genesis 1:26–28). God could have created something completely inconsistent with Himself, but He didn't. No, He created man in His own image. In the way parents give birth to children in their image, so God created man and woman in His own image. And like the DNA shared by a family that not only carries with it physical attributes but also emotional, intellectual, and spiritual characteristics, God created man and woman like Himself. **We were designed in the image of God.** And so, like God, you have a mind that is capable of rational thought, you can make decisions, create, communicate, be social, love, and care for others. Humans were given sovereignty over all the creation that was lower than us (Genesis 1:28–30). We have the ability to build things, to write songs, to understand math and science. Like God, who is the eternal Spirit, you too have a spirit. And with that spirit you can worship and relate to Him. So God gave Himself to humanity the way parents give themselves, their very nature, to their children.

# THE NATURE OF GOD

*Knowing who God is helps you to better understand why He does what He does and what He wants for your life. Here is a list of some of the attributes of God.*

## GOD IS:

**Eternal/Infinite:** Psalm 90:2; Isaiah 46:8–10

**Omniscient/All-knowing**: Psalm 139:2–4; Proverbs 15:3; Hebrews 4:13

**Omnipotent/All-powerful:** Isaiah 40:22–23; Jeremiah 32:17

**Omnipresent/Always present:** Psalm 139:7–10; Proverbs 15:3

**Love:** Ephesians 2:4; 2 Corinthians 13:11; 1 John 4:8

**Faithful:** 1 Peter 4:19; Hebrews 11:11

**Merciful:** Romans 9:16

**Kind** (*Kindness* is another word for *grace*): Romans 2:4; 1 Corinthians 15:10; Ephesians 2:8

# GOD IS: (CONT.)

**Righteous:** Psalm 11:7; Psalm 145:17

**Just:** Genesis 18:25; 1 Peter 2:23

**Perfect:** Psalm 18:30; Matthew 5:48

**Self-sufficient:** Psalm 50:12; Isaiah 40:28

**Sovereign:** Deuteronomy 10:14; Proverbs 16:9; James 4:15

**Holy:** Exodus 15:11; Isaiah 6:3

**Good:** Exodus 33:18–19; Psalm 31:19; Psalm 100:5

**Jealous:** Exodus 34:14; Psalm 78:58; James 4:4–5

**Truth:** Isaiah 65:16; John 14:6

**Wise:** Proverbs 3:19; 1 Corinthians 1:18–25; Colossians 2:3

**Incomprehensible:** Job 11:7–9; Psalm 18:11

But **there are a few things in His nature that God didn't give to us as His human children.** Some aspects of His nature are not a part of ours, like omnipresence or self-sufficiency. We all have needs that we can't meet on our own. **None of us can create something from nothing.** We can't create the plants or animals we need for food. We can grow them from something God already created, but we can't create them. We can't make the earth move around the sun, or keep the ocean from overflowing. There is plenty in life to prove the fact that we are not self-sufficient, and that we need not only other human beings but God Himself in order to live life to the full, let alone to live at all.

In fact, you not only need God for your physical well-being, but your spiritual health as well. See; **one of the unmistakable things about God is His absolute perfection, His holiness, His sinlessness.** As you can see in 1 Samuel 2:2, *"There is no one holy like the LORD. There is no one besides You! And there is no rock like our God."* All of God's power, all His decisions, all His actions, all of His nature has, at its root, His holiness. And that's a good thing, because without that this world would be a place with no hope. But His holiness is what explains His perfect goodness and not evil, His complete kindness and not cruelty, His pure perfection and not flaw.

But let's define *holiness* really quickly, since it's probably not a word you use every day. **Holiness is the description of sinlessness.** It literally means set apart. He is so perfect, so pure, so unevil that He is set apart from everything and everyone else. In fact, **He is so holy that His holiness can't tolerate the presence of evil. After all, if there were any evil in Him, then He would no longer be perfectly holy.** Knowing this about Him is crucial, because out of His holiness comes every bit of His nature. That means that everything you know about Him must be looked at through the light of His sinlessness. So **He doesn't do anything that is evil.** Even the things He does that we can't understand are not evil, but for the ultimate good of man. In Him there is no darkness (1 John 1:5), no evil, no sin. All His ways are perfect, all His actions are pure and good, He is holy, and so is everything He does. In Psalm 145:17 it says, *"The Lord is righteous in all His ways and gracious in all His acts."* That means that **nothing but the best can come from Him.** His holiness is behind all of His actions, all of His power of creation, and all of His laws. In Genesis 1:31 this idea is explained when God calls everything that He made "good." And because God made Adam and Eve and walked with them and talked with them, you can know that a relationship with Him is what you were made for. As a child of Adam and Eve, made in the image of God, you were created to be with God, here on the earth and long after you leave this earth. And because He is holy, you can know that this relationship is safe. He isn't out to destroy you or to trick you. He isn't a distant father figure who only shows up every other weekend. He is a perfect, sinless, pure God who will only do what is best for you. He loves you and will never leave you or forsake you (Deuteronomy 31:6). He is the perfect one for you! And He made you for Himself. Just like He couldn't give us His endlessness, omnipotence, or omnipresence, He couldn't give us His holiness or perfection. That would make you like God, which, as you will see in the next chapter, is the very thing that Adam and Eve (Genesis 3:6), and even Satan (Isaiah 14:12–20) were all longing for when they fell.

**God will give you His holiness, but it's made possible through His suffering, not your effort; through His life and your death of self-interest.**

But we are getting ahead of ourselves. Just know that your obedience and pursuit of holiness should flow out of gratitude and love, not a need to earn salvation or approval. Your pursuit of holiness is empowered, not by how good you are but by Christ in you. And that is the most important part of the whole big picture idea: **this life isn't about you and what you**

**accomplish through your own try-hard strength, but about Him and what He's already accomplished in His holiness.**

This can be a hard pill to swallow. After all, you are used to managing your own life, working hard to get good grades, to get a good job, to get attention or success. But the life of faith breaks the mold of the try-hard life. Chances are that all your life you've wanted the freedom to do whatever you wanted to do and work however hard you wanted to work. The older you got the more you said, "I can do it myself." Freedom is something everybody inherently wants. But **true freedom belongs to only one person, to God Himself.** The rest of us are limited in our freedom, as the singer/songwriter Bob Dylan once said:

*"No one is free.*
*Even the birds are chained to the sky."*

And it's true, not even wild animals are free. Most people think of birds as flying free, but the truth is that birds are anything but free. After all, they have to live in a specific region all the days of their lives, doing just what they were made to do. Their instincts drive their actions, not their freedom. They have to hunt continually to feed themselves, they are slaves to their nature. And it's the same with you. **You are not free to do whatever you want, no matter what you think. If you**

**were, then you would be like God.** His freedom is a part of His nature and is why He was free to create man however He wanted, and it's why man can't judge God or accuse Him of making a mistake in creation. As it says in Romans 9:20–21, *"Who are you, a mere man, to talk back to God? Will what is formed say to the one who formed it, 'Why did you make me like this?' Or has the potter no right over the clay, to make from the same lump one piece of pottery for honor and another for dishonor?"*

**But His divine freedom, the ability to do whatever He pleases, is not a part of your nature.** Because of our sin nature, we are not free to be sinless, however much we'd like to be. **No one is free not to sin, so no one is completely free.** That means that you don't have complete freedom, as God does. Because, after all, Psalm 115:3 says, *"Our God is in heaven and does whatever He pleases."* If humans had complete freedom, then someone, over the span of all time, would have at some point been perfect. There have been many who have tried to be perfect, who have wanted it more than anything. But still, there hasn't been any human outside of Jesus who was perfect, and so the human race has lived chained to the inevitability of sin and its consequences, though Christ's death on the cross frees believers from sin's eternal consequences.

# GOD'S NATURE GIVES HIM THE FREEDOM TO DO WHATEVER HE WANTS TO DO.

*God is supreme, He is ruler of all, and that is what gives Him divine freedom. As it says in Psalm 24:1,* "The earth and everything in it, the world and its inhabitants, belong to the Lord." *He is self-existent, He doesn't report to anyone (Isaiah 40:2). He's free from space and time, so He can go where He wants to go, do what He wants to do. And while this can be scary to the uninformed or the unbelieving, to the Christian this should be relief. It means that* **God can't be redirected or removed from you by any force, not even by Satan.** *A lot of people give Satan a lot more credit than he deserves, blaming him for their misery, their closed doors, broken dreams, or terrifying circumstances. But this idea flies in the face of God's freedom. God is the only free person alive.* **Not even Satan is free to do what God doesn't want him to do.** *Though he may roam the world looking for souls to devour, he is only allowed to do so by our all-powerful, all-knowing God.*

**No one pressures God to do what they want Him to do against His will.** He does whatever He wants when He wants. That means no one can pressure Him to punish you, to hurt you, or to ignore you. No one can successfully pray to God against you. God will not be pressured to act against His own nature, because He can't act in a way that is inconsistent with Himself (see Hebrews 1:12). And that's important for you to understand, because it means that God can be trusted. He doesn't do things that are evil or imperfect, but only what is good, because He by nature is good (see Psalm 25:8). So even though you aren't free to not sin, in His freedom He can and does give you the power to be holy because He is holy (see Leviticus 11:44). But this holiness, that comes from God Himself, is nothing you can brag about because it's not anything you do outside of God's power that is Christ living in you.

Bet you never knew you could learn so much about God from just taking a closer look at creation. But **God's nature is unchangeable**, and learning who He was in the beginning will give you the same answer as learning who He is today and will be tomorrow. He cannot change. **If He changed, He would have to go from good to bad or from good to better, both of which would make Him imperfect either by falling or by needing to climb to a higher nature.** Both of which are impossible.

That's another bit of good news for His creation. It means He isn't inconsistent in His thoughts, actions, or words, but that He is firm, a solid foundation to build not only your faith but your life on as well.

# GOD WITH US IN THE GARDEN

After God created Adam and Eve, He gave them Himself in a tangible walking-around kind of way. He actually spent time with them. He talked to them, He was *with* them in person (see Genesis 3:8). The story of creation isn't a story of some distant God who made everything and then went away, but the story of an infinite, perfect, all-powerful, loving God who made man for the expressed purpose of being with Him, of giving all that is His glory to His children. **The fact that God walked with Adam and Eve means that He wanted companionship with them.** And this is an amazing thing: that the perfect, all-powerful God of the universe would want to spend time talking and walking with man is unfathomable, but true. And it is because of the story of creation that you can know He wants a relationship with you. This is the ultimate answer to what your purpose on the earth is: to be in a love relationship with God.

But your life is nothing like the garden. Your life is hard, there are trials and tribulations. You have tons of unanswered questions like

"Why me?" and "How could He?" You want to see things more clearly, but life doesn't always make sense. When you have more questions than answers, you can become overwhelmed. When the focus of your life is the unknown, when it's the work you have to do in order to be happy, or the failure you have to live with because of your own weaknesses, life becomes a hot mess. As you focus on yourself, as you worry about yourself, plan for yourself, work for yourself, yourself fails you and the world around you rises up to beat you down. In fact, it could be said that all the problems in your heart and mind are the result of your life being out of focus. That's because

**when you concentrate on anything or anyone other than God, you end up worshipping something or someone who is not perfect, powerful, holy, or free. Where you put your focus, you put your faith.**

You end up serving the creation rather than the Creator. And that is a formula for failure, because the creation you serve will never ever love you or give to you the way God will. But choosing to make Him the focus of your life, to keep Him as the main thing, is to choose hope, freedom, and the best for your life. *The Big Picture* is so much more than a catchy title, it's a perspective on life that will give you the answers you've been looking for, and not only the answers, but the joy and peace that you deeply long for.

# DISCUSSION QUESTIONS:

*Why did God create people?*

*How does that affect your purpose?*

*In what ways should you being an image bearer of God affect the way you live?*

*What are some of God's attributes that He didn't give His creation, in other words the ones that only belong to God?*

*Why is it a good thing that He didn't share those attributes?*

*What does Lamentations 3:37–38 teach you about God?*

*What are some reasons that it might be good that God didn't give humans total freedom to do whatever they wanted?*

# OTHER RESOURCES:

*The God Who is There*, D. A. Carson (2010)

*The Knowledge of the Holy*, A. W. Tozer (1961)

If you want to look into God's glory for yourself, find out about His attributes, those things that make up His very nature. Here are some resources that you can read for free online:

*The Attributes of God*, by A. W. Pink (Public Domain, Google it)

## Podcasts:

Mark Dever: *"Understanding the Story Line of the Bible"*
http://thegospelcoalition.org/resources/a/understanding_the_
story_line_of_the_bible

David Landrith: *"The Gospel According to Genesis"*
http://www.longhollow.com/messages/series/44?media=audio&
message=372

You can find more podcasts like these at: www.gospelproject.
com/additionalresources.

# CHAPTER 2
# JESUS WITH YOU

*Make your own attitude that of Christ Jesus, who, existing in the form of God, did not consider equality with God as something to be used for His own advantage. Instead He emptied Himself by assuming the form of a slave, taking on the likeness of men. And when He had come as a man in His external form, He humbled Himself by becoming obedient to the point of death— even to death on a cross.* (Philippians 2:5–8)

Where did it all go wrong? When did life spiral out of control? And when did failure become an option for the human race? In the beginning, God gave us a perfect world. He entered into it and hung out with our first parents. It was pure perfection. But that soon came to a screeching halt when the creation was faced with the chance to become like the Creator. Heaven on the earth wasn't enough. Eve wanted more. So when the serpent said eating the fruit would give her more knowledge, though she knew God had forbidden it (Genesis 2:16–17), she took a bite. She believed the lie of the serpent that accused God of exaggerating the punishment just to keep her from becoming like Him. She accepted God's love and kindness and threw out His justice and judgment, all so that she could be in the know. Not only that, but she handed the fruit to her husband and he took a bite as well, and the die was cast. Life was forever altered. Man's intimate relationship with God was broken. In fact, it was cut so badly that God sent them away. He locked them out of the garden and gave them a death sentence: a physical death sentence because they wouldn't have access to the tree of life any longer, so they would one day actually die; but also a spiritual death because they would be separated from God. (If you haven't read it in a while, you should take a look at the whole story in Genesis 3.)

# SIN KILLS

So **death came into the world through the sin of Adam and Eve.** According to Romans 6:16, sin leads to death. And James 1:15 says that when sin is fully grown it gives birth to death. Adam and Eve knew what God told His people later in Romans 6:23: "The wages of sin is death." So death it was. And not only theirs, but yours and ours as well. See,

**when the original parents sinned, they did it for all of us, meaning their sin became a part of every other human being's life.**

They are, after all, our parents. Like it says in Romans 5:12, *"Just as sin entered the world through one man [Adam], and death through sin, in this way death spread to all men [including you], because all sinned."* Original sin means that all mankind, because of Adam and Eve, are not only destined to die a physical death but are born sinful, or spiritually dead, and so are separated from God. As it says in Romans 3:10, "There is no one righteous, not even one." So the God that was with us in the garden, because of sin, suddenly stops walking around with us and puts us out into the hard, cold world to labor and toil, separated from fellowship with Him. End of story? Not even. In fact, this all happens within the first 3 chapters of the Bible. **The rest of the Bible becomes the story of mankind's restoration or return to relationship with God.** The first peek at this restoration happens in Genesis 3:21, where we see the literal and quick death of the animals whose skins God used to cover Adam and Eve's naked bodies. This isn't just a throw away verse. It's the beginning of, or the foreshadowing of, the most important thing in the history of mankind: the death of Jesus on the cross. The blood of these animals, and all of the animals that were sacrificed after them, was a temporary covering and appeasement to God that reinforced the nature of sin. **In order to come into the presence of God as a sinful human being, your sinfulness has to be covered by the blood of an innocent.** And before Christ came to the earth and walked with us, animal life represented "innocence." This sacrificial system of forgiveness of sins taught mankind the destructiveness of sin and God's hatred of it. For the people who lived in the BC era, the blood flowed daily. And because of that men were able to have a relationship with God.

# JESUS IN THE OLD TESTAMENT

**This sacrificial system set the stage for the arrival of Jesus**, because the blood of the animals covered sins only temporarily, not forever. Each day more blood was shed to cover each day's sins. When you read all this stuff that seems so foreign to you as a modern human being, it helps to look at it as a promise of the ultimate sacrifice, Jesus. In the book of Hebrews, it says this of Jesus,

> He entered the most holy place once for all, not by the blood of goats and calves, but by His own blood, having obtained eternal redemption. For if the blood of goats and bulls and the ashes of a young cow, sprinkling those who are defiled, sanctify for the purification of the flesh, how much more will the blood of the Messiah, who through the eternal Spirit offered Himself without blemish to God, cleanse our consciences from dead works to serve the living God? (Hebrews 9:12–14)

And in Hebrews 10:4, we realized that this sacrificial system before Christ was truly an appeasement to God, not a permanent solution, because of this statement: "For it is impossible for the blood of bulls and goats to take away sins."

We can get a glimpse of this sacrificial system in the Old Testament when we look at the life of Abraham and his son Isaac.

Isaac was the child that God promised Abraham he would have in his old age, the child He promised would be the father of a nation. So when God asked Abraham to sacrifice Isaac on the altar, you can imagine the pain and confusion Abraham felt. But still he went. He took his son to Mount Moriah and laid his innocent child on an altar, strapped him down, and raised the knife to kill him. And while this story is true, it isn't only what it seems. It also shows us a glimpse at Abraham as God the Father and Isaac as the son, Jesus, being laid out for sacrifice. And as Isaac was lifted off the altar and lived on, so Jesus was raised from the dead and lives today.

**Time and time again you can see throughout the Old Testament the life of Jesus foreshadowed, revealing that His coming was always the plan, always the necessity.**

Even after centuries of trying to do it right, to be good, and to live by the law, no human being has been able to do it. So the blood kept flowing, and the people waited for a more suitable sacrifice. This is a really amazing perspective, because it makes the Old Testament the story of Jesus and His relationship with mankind. It shows us that Jesus was with us always, always preparing the way, always reminding us that he was enough, always giving us an understanding of our complete inability to be good, and that

His complete love would make a way for our relationship with Him even without our own perfection.

Reading the Old Testament should never be just about the events and the people themselves. It should always give you insight into God's desire to have a relationship with His children and the certainty that He would one day give us an eternal sacrifice worthy of cleansing us from everything we have ever done, or ever will do. See, God isn't watching from afar, but He's working His will and His way throughout all of history. And He's making a way for His children to be with Him.

From the beginning of creation Jesus is there. **In Genesis 3:15, His coming to the earth is promised** when it says the seed of woman will bruise the serpent's head; that seed is Jesus and the serpent is Satan. Then He is seen as **the Passover lamb** spoken of in Exodus 12:5 where God says to the Israelites, *"You must have an unblemished animal, a year-old male; you may take it from either the sheep or the goats."* This Passover lamb was the lamb that was killed and its blood put on the front doors of their houses, so that the angel of death would pass over their homes when he came to kill all of the firstborn sons in Egypt—just as Jesus would be the lamb that would be killed in order to save the lives of those who accept His blood over their sin. Later, the Passover became a yearly ritual that was celebrated by God's people. And each year a lamb was killed at twilight, or "between the two evenings" (see Exodus 12:6), which is between 3:00 and 5:00 p.m., without any bones being broken (see Exodus 12:46). And that's just what happened to Jesus. He died at twilight (see Matthew 27:46) and His bones were never broken (see John 19:33).

When the Israelites were wandering in the desert for forty years, they found it hard to find enough food to feed them all, so they complained to God about it. And God responded by giving them **manna** to eat. Manna was a kind of flaked bread that gave them all they needed for nourishment. And **it is a symbol of Christ Himself,** who we later see is the bread of life, all that we need to live as you can see in John 6:32–33, when Jesus says, *"'I assure you: Moses didn't give you the bread from heaven, but My Father gives you the real bread from heaven. For the bread of God is the One who comes down from heaven and gives life to the world.' Then they said, 'Sir, give us this bread always!'"* (John 6:32–34).

Not only that, but the people also needed something to drink. After all, there's not much water in the desert. God provided for them by giving them something—a rock. What?! How could they get water from a rock? Well, check it out. *"'I am going to stand there in front of you on the rock at Horeb; when you hit the rock, water will come out of it and the people will drink.' Moses did this in the sight of the elders of Israel"* (Exodus 17:6). And maybe you guessed this already, but **that rock was a symbol of Jesus Himself,** who is called the rock in 1 Corinthians 10:4 and described as being "struck," or "smitten" in some translations, in Isaiah 53:4. So the bread and the rock both show up in the Old Testament as a shadow of the real bread and rock to come in the form of Jesus.

The next book, Leviticus, might seem like a tedious list of rules and regulations, but it is a vivid picture of how much God detests sin and its effect on humanity. It is meant to help you understand how impossible it is to be holy by your own will power and strength, by being good and obeying all the law, as it says in James 2:10: *"Whoever keeps the entire law, yet fails in one point, is guilty of breaking it all."* You can't be good enough in your own strength to keep all of the law. There is just too much of it to follow, and this proves the need for a Savior, for someone who can take on your sins so that the Father can see you as pure and innocent and can have an eternal relationship with you. So **Leviticus is that huge reminder of sin and how much it costs, and that the blood and death involved are too much for you to bear without Christ.** But it is also in Leviticus that we first see the Day of Atonement. In this yearly ritual, one animal was sacrificed as a sin offering to God and another was touched by all the priests who confessed the sins of the people over it. They then took the living goat and led it away into the wilderness (Leviticus 16:21–22). So the sacrificed goat or "scapegoat" represented the death and the atoning blood of Jesus (see Hebrews 9:11–12), while the other represented His resurrection and the complete removal of our sins (see Isaiah 53:4, 6, and John 1:29).

# MICHAEL'S LITTLE PICTURE

*When I was seventeen, I said a prayer and accepted Jesus into my heart, and that was that. To me it was the magic prayer, my fire insurance. I didn't look back, and I certainly didn't think about how much God hates sin. So there I was, over a decade later, gambling in order to get some kind of control in my life. And before I knew it, I was out of cash. Since I had access to the petty cash at work, I dipped into it and took some of it to play the tables at the local casino. Here I was, supposedly a Christian, not paying an ounce of attention to how much God hates sin and loves me. Instead, I accepted the lie that His love wasn't enough, so I let the petty cash and my gambling try to be enough. But soon that petty cash ran out, and I ended up under arrest, sitting in a jail cell, looking at four walls and a Bible. It all came crashing down on me—the awareness of my messed up life and my need for a Savior, not just from eventual hell and fire but immediately from myself. From my own weakness, emptiness, and self-obsession. My sin and me minimizing God's love and grace had decimated not only my life, but the lives of those I love. God is right in His hatred of sin, and so on that fateful day I agreed with Him. But I also agreed with Him that Jesus' sacrifice was enough to cover all that sin and His love would propel me to obedience instead of me trying to be enough for Him on my own. And since I saw myself for the sinner that I truly am and saw Christ as the Savior He truly is, I have experienced freedom in giving up control to God and have never looked back.*

Dr. H. G. Guinness puts it this way, "To understand the seriousness of sin, we must fathom three oceans, the ocean of human suffering, the ocean of the sufferings of the Lord Jesus Christ, the ocean of future suffering which awaits impenitent sinners."

# In order for you to truly grasp your need for Jesus, you first have to understand the depth of sin.

And that was one of the purposes of the law, to reveal sin. Romans 3:20 explains this idea better: *"For no one will be justified in His sight by the works of the law, because the knowledge of sin comes through the law."* Everyone sins; but it's only those who recognize their sin by seeing it in the Word of God who are even aware of their need for salvation. After all, if you didn't know you were sinful, if you weren't aware of your imperfections, of your selfishness or pride, then you would never look for Jesus. You would never even consider giving your life to Him because you wouldn't see a need for Him. **The Old Testament helps you identify your impurity and inability to**

**be perfect like Christ.** It also shows you how important your holiness is to God and how powerless you are to achieve it. As you saw in Romans 3:20, you cannot be justified by the works of the law, by getting them all right, you just can't. So there has to be another answer, and that answer is Jesus.

**Jesus is seen throughout the book of Leviticus in the types of offerings given.** An offering, or sacrifice, was a gift that the people gave to atone for their sins, and the offering itself represents Christ. We see this in Hebrews 9:14: *"How much more will the blood of the Messiah, who through the eternal Spirit offered Himself without blemish to God, cleanse our consciences from dead works to serve the living God?"* But not only an offering, Christ is also seen in the person of the priests spoken of so much in this book, as you can see in Hebrews 4:14: *"Therefore, since we have a great high priest who has passed through the heavens—Jesus the Son of God—let us hold fast to the confession."* So Leviticus is filled with pointers not only to the life of Jesus, but also to the ultimate sacrifice of Jesus as the final atonement for your sins.

This often skipped-over book has within its pages an awful lot of talk about the blood. And that's one of the things that makes it so very important. Without blood a creature dies. Blood is the life force of an animal, and because of that it is an acceptable sacrifice for sin, as it says in Leviticus 17:11: *"For the life of a creature is in the blood, and I have appointed it to you to make atonement on the altar for your lives, since it is the lifeblood that makes atonement."*

In the next book, the book of Numbers, you get to see how God lived with the Israelites in the desert. After they escaped slavery in Egypt, God told them to build a tabernacle for Him to live in. And in that tabernacle, you see another shadow of Christ. The tabernacle, also called the tent of meeting, was described like this by God Himself: *"They are to make a sanctuary for Me so that I may dwell among them"* (Exodus 25:8). This is something that's echoed in the New Testament as well. John 1:14 says, *"The Word became flesh and took up residence among us."* So **the tabernacle was the place where God lived with man in order to have relationship with His people, which is a foreshadowing of Christ living with us here on the earth.**

After the Israelites built the tabernacle in the desert, it was covered by a cloud during the day and a fire at night, so that everyone could see in the darkness (See Numbers 9:15). **The cloud was God's presence with His people and a symbol of Jesus as a light in the darkness**.

You can see Him talking about Himself as this light in John 8:12: *"Then Jesus spoke to them again: 'I am the light of the world. Anyone who follows Me will never walk in the darkness but will have the light of life.'"* That this pillar of cloud and light was in fact the very presence of Jesus is seen in Exodus 14:19: *"Then the Angel of God, who was going in front of the Israelite forces, moved and went behind them. The pillar of cloud moved from in front of them and stood behind them."* **The "Angel of God" is the description of the Son of God before He became a man.** From this you can see the Son of God involved with His people on the earth, guiding His people, protecting them, and meeting with them.

This is seen very clearly in the life of Moses. Moses, the one to whom God gave the law in the form of the Ten Commandments, is meant to symbolize the uselessness of people trying to be perfect by trying harder, by following the law, and working at being good enough for God. Both Moses and Jesus were children when the ruler at the time commanded that all baby boys were to be killed (Exodus 1:15–16; Matthew 2:16). They both left the palace of the king to save their people (Hebrews 11:24; Hebrews 1:2). And they both offered their lives to save the people (Exodus 32:30–33; 2 Corinthians 5:15). Moses is the prophet of the old covenant and

Jesus is the prophet of the new, and they were the only ones to actually see God face-to-face (Exodus 20:21; Matthew 11:27). And while there are also some big differences, with Moses being 100 percent human and making mistakes (since he was 0 percent God), and Jesus being perfect in all His ways, being both 100 percent God and 100 percent human, Jesus is still seen as the promised one by Moses in Deuteronomy 18:15, where he says, *"The Lord your God will raise up for you a **prophet like me** from among your own brothers. You must listen to him."* We could go on and on showing you the foreshadowing and pointers to the life of Christ and His death and resurrection seen in the Old Testament. We could even go on and on showing you time after time when He came to the earth and showed Himself to men, before He was ever a baby in a manger. In fact, **every time you see "the Angel of God" appearing to people in the Old Testament, you are seeing what is called a *Christophany*, or an appearance of the preincarnate Christ on the earth.** You can see Him appearing all over the Old Testament, sometimes as a man and sometimes in a burning bush or pillar of cloud, sometimes as an Angel of God, but you see Christophanies happen time and again as evidence that Jesus has always been with us on the earth. **He isn't a distant figure, removed from the**

**fray and watching you like a man watching a movie with a big bowl of popcorn on His lap.** No, Jesus is continually showing up in the lives of men to save them. Like the time in the book of Daniel when He joined the three Jewish boys who had been throw into the fiery furnace for failing to worship another god. Three were thrown in the fire, but four were seen together in the flames. The fourth was the Son of God, and because of His presence the boys didn't burn up in the fire. In fact, they didn't even smell of smoke when they walked out.

A lot of times people look at the Old Testament and see a completely different God than the one in the New Testament. They see a God of wrath and wars, and they wonder why He's so different from Jesus. But it's the same God.

**If you look more closely at the Old Testament, you will see that not only is He the same God, but He was actively involved in saving, protecting, speaking, and living with His people long before He became a man and dwelled among us.**

This is important, because it can change the way you think about your life. If your life feels more Old Testament than New, then it's time to **start looking for the evidences of Christ's work in your life.** Look around and find the instances where God saved you, interceded for you, or put you on a path. Just like Christ is all over the Old Testament, He is all over your life as well. It's just that sometimes you don't realize it. But knowing His hands are all over the entirety of history should be a confirmation that they are all over your life as well. You are a part of the big picture of God; He hasn't changed His nature in our day. He isn't acting differently or becoming more distant. He is moving among us and is still sovereign over all. Knowing that He is an actively involved God can either scare you or give you peace, depending on how you live. Either way, it's time to begin to see the big picture and to stop pretending that He isn't a God who is pursuing a relationship with you.

Rather than going on for pages more showing you the evidences of Jesus from every book of the Old Testament, here is a list of a few more instances of Jesus coming to the earth in the Old Testament, Christophonies, or verses that foreshadow Him coming soon. Then look at the list on pages 53–55.

*In the Old Testament Jesus is:*

| | | |
|---|---|---|
| Genesis | The Angel of the Lord | Gen. 12:7–9; 16:7–11; 18:1–33; 22:11–18, 33:22–30 |
| Exodus | The Angel of God, The Passover Lamb, The Angel of the Lord, | Exod. 3:2–6; 12:3; 14:19 |
| Leviticus | The Atonement | Lev. 16 |
| Numbers | The Angel of the Lord | Num. 22:22–35, |
| Deuteronomy | The City of Refuge | Deut. 19; 21:23 |
| Joshua | The Commander of the army of the Lord | Josh. 5:13–15 |
| Judges | The Angel of the Lord, The Angel of God | Judg. 2:1–4; 5:23; 6:11–12; 6:20–22; 13:3–21 |
| Ruth | | |
| 1 Samuel | The Rock, The Lord | 1 Sam. 2:2, 10 |
| 2 Samuel | The Angel of the Lord | 2 Sam. 24:16 |
| 1 Kings | The Angel of the Lord | 1 Kings 19:7 |
| 2 Kings | The Angel of the Lord | 2 Kings 1:3: 1:15: 19:35 |
| 1 Chronicles | The Angel of the Lord, A better David* | 1 Chron. 21:15; 21:18 |
| 2 Chronicles | A better King Hezekiah | 2 Chron. 29 |

| | | |
|---|---|---|
| Ezra | Zerubbabel (Master Builder), chief cornerstone or capstone | Ezra 4:3; Zec. 4:7–9 |
| Nehemiah | A better Nehemiah*, Governor of Judah, man of prayer | Neh. 5:14; Matt. 2:6 |
| Esther | A better Esther*, Intercessor for God's people | Jesus not only risked His life, but gave His life for God's people, and now he intercedes for all of us; Rom. 8:34 |
| Job | A better Job*, suffered, fully submitted to God | Jesus is an innocent who suffered and intercedes for His friends |
| Psalm | The Angel of the Lord | Ps. 34:7 |
| Proverbs | Wisdom | Prov. 8:22–23; 1 Cor. 1:24; Col. 2:3 |
| Ecclesiastes | The Preacher, King, and Son of David | Eccles. 1:1 |
| Song of Solomon | The Groom (The bride's beloved) | Jesus is the bridegroom; Song of Solomon |
| Isaiah | The Angel of the Lord, Immanuel, Man of Sorrows, | Isa. 11:1; 37:36; 7:14; 53:3 |
| Jeremiah | A Righteous Branch, Branch of Righteousness, A better Jeremiah | Jer. 23:5–6; 33:15–16 |
| Lamentations | A better Jeremiah* (the weeping prophet) | the whole book of Lamentations is connected with the deep sufferings of Jeremiah, because Israel and Jerusalem were destroyed. |

| | | |
|---|---|---|
| Ezekiel | A better Ezekiel* the Shepherd | Ezek. 34:23 |
| Daniel | The Angel | Dan. 3:25–28 |
| Hosea | A better Hosea* | Hos. 3 |
| Joel | The Lord | Joel 2:32 |
| Amos | The tabernacle of David | Amos 9:11–12 |
| Obadiah | Salvation of Zion | Obad. 1:17 |
| Jonah | A better Jonah* | Jesus was cast out into the storm so that we could be saved; Jonah 1:17 |
| Micah | Ruler in Israel | Mic. 5:2 |
| Nahum | A better Nahum | Nahum announced God's judgment on sin, Jesus takes the sins of the world onto Himself |
| Habakkuk | The redemptive act of Salvation | Hab. 3:13–14 |
| Zephaniah | Grace | Zeph. 3:15–17; foreshadows the grace of Christ |
| Haggai | A better Governor and High Priest* | Hag. 1:14–2:5 |
| Zechariah | Angel of the Lord, The Branch, the Shepherd | Zech 1:11; 3:8; 13:7 |
| Malachi | The Refiner, The Sun of Righteousness | Mal. 3:3; 4:2 |

(Note: *When we say Jesus is "a better" blank, we mean that the person gives you a picture of what Christ will do when He walks the earth. In other words, He rebuilds the temple [i.e., the Church body], He saves His people, weeps for His people, etc.)

These foreshadowings or "types" of Jesus (theologians call them archtypes,) make the Old Testament a constant witness to the life of Christ and a promise of His coming in the flesh.

**You will never read the Old Testament the same again once you learn that Christ's fingerprints and life are all over it.**

All the moments where God is actively involved in history, even when things look like things are the worst they've ever been, show that He is still there. That's important in your life because it is meant to help you understand that no matter how crazy things look, no matter how bad things get, Jesus is there. He isn't ignoring you and your situation. He isn't powerless to help. In fact, He is working to accomplish His perfect and loving will in your life. We know this, not just because He is all over the Old Testament, but also because the Old Testament promises Him as Messiah, the chosen one, sent to save His people and deliver us all from the grip of the enemy.

# THE PROPHETS: GOD'S SPOKESMEN

After Adam and Eve were kicked out of the garden, God didn't walk with them anymore, but He did talk to a handful of men and women who were called prophets. **God used these prophets to speak for Him.** He would speak to them, like He did with Moses through the burning bush, and then these men and women would speak to the rest of the people about what they heard God say. So there was access to God, but it was through an intermediary. God gave these people special abilities; abilities that allowed them to do things like interpret dreams, part seas, and protect His people. God hand-picked these people; it wasn't like they were voted into power or anything. It didn't matter who they were or where they came from, they were all different. What mattered was that they listened to God and He sent them.

So, **God was also with us in the Old Testament through the prophets.** The people looked to the prophets for all they needed to know. Part of the reason for this is seen in the book of Exodus. When God appeared at Mt. Sinai to Moses and all the people He had led out of Egypt, they freaked out. Take a look at the panic in Exodus 20:18–19, *"All the people witnessed the thunder and lightning, the* *sound of the trumpet, and the mountain surrounded by smoke. When the people saw it they trembled and stood at a distance. 'You speak to us, and we will listen,' they said to Moses, 'but don't let God speak to us, or we will die.'"* God's power was so amazing it scared the people half to death, so they asked for an intermediary. They wanted Moses to talk to God and then tell them what He said. So Moses went up to the top of Mt. Sinai to be the intermediary between the people and God. Moses then helped the Israelites to understand who God was and what He wanted for them. Moses was actually in the presence of God (see Exodus 34:5). He didn't get a phone call or hear from an angel, he was in the actual presence of God, here on the earth. After going to the top of Mt. Sinai and getting the Ten Commandments, Moses' face still glowed when he came back down, so amazing was the presence of God (see Exodus 34:35). You might know the feeling, if only in a tiny way, when you are with someone you love more than anything and your face gets all flushed just from being in his or her presence. This is just a speck of how amazing it was for Moses to be in the presence of God.

Other prophets like Jeremiah, Zachariah, and Isaiah told the people about the future. They told them when God was angry and was about to punish them. They gave them a chance to change, as Jonah reluctantly did for the Ninevites (Jonah 3). And they told the people about the coming Messiah, the Savior. How He would be born, where He would live, and what He would do. Their prophecies helped the Israelites know God's will and God's plans for His children. The prophets were the access the people had to God here on the earth.

Their prophecies are jam-packed into the pages of the Old Testament, like chips into mint chocolate chip ice cream. And they were meant to make the people ready for when the Messiah would come. They were ready, because after seeing generation after generation fail to obey the law and honor God they, like Hayley did so long ago, could begin to say, "We can't do it alone. We're not good enough." And the idea of savior began to make sense to them. The prophecies showed them what their *Savior* would do, but also what man would do to Him. Because they predicted things that would happen in the future, the people didn't have an excuse for not believing that Jesus was who He said He was when the prophesied events occurred.

**Because of all of the prophecies about Him, we can see without a doubt that Jesus is more than just another prophet. He is the Son of God;** God Himself in the flesh. After all, generations spoke of His coming and were prepared to accept Him as their Messiah. In Isaiah 7:14, the virgin birth of Jesus is prophesied, and, of course, it was fulfilled in the life of Christ who was born in Bethlehem as promised in Micah 5:2, and from the ancestry of David as foretold in Isaiah 11:1,10 and Jeremiah 23:5. The Bible also makes promises about the coming Messiah that make it impossible for anyone else to claim to be Him. Isaiah 35:5 promises miracles He will work when *"The eyes of the blind will be opened, and the ears of the deaf unstopped"* (see Isaiah 35:5–6), which were fulfilled many times in the life of Christ. Here's one in John 9:6–7: *"After He said these things He spit on the ground, made some mud from the saliva, and spread the mud on his eyes. 'Go,' He told him, 'wash in the pool of Siloam' (which means 'Sent'). So he left, washed, and came back seeing."*

# THE PROMISE OF THE COMING MESSIAH, THE PROPHECY OF JESUS FROM ISAIAH

Who has believed what we have heard? And who has the arm of the LORD been revealed to? He grew up before Him like a young plant and like a root out of dry ground. He didn't have an impressive form or majesty that we should look at Him, no appearance that we should desire Him. He was despised and rejected by men, a man of suffering who knew what sickness was. He was like someone people turned away from; He was despised, and we didn't value Him. Yet He Himself bore our sicknesses, and He carried our pains; but we in turn regarded Him stricken, struck down by God, and afflicted. But He was pierced because of our transgressions, crushed because of our iniquities; punishment for our peace was on Him, and we are healed by His wounds. We all went astray like sheep; we all have turned to our own way; and the LORD has punished Him for the iniquity of us all. He was oppressed and afflicted, yet He did not open His mouth. Like a lamb led to the slaughter and like a sheep silent before her shearers, He did not open His mouth. He was taken away because of oppression and judgment; and who considered His fate? For He was cut off from the land of the living; He was struck because of my people's rebellion. They made His grave with the wicked and with a rich man at His death, although He had done no violence and had not spoken deceitfully. Yet the LORD was pleased to crush Him severely. When You make Him a restitution offering, He will see His seed, He will prolong His days, and by His hand, the LORD's pleasure will be accomplished. He will see it out of His anguish, and He will be satisfied with His knowledge. My righteous Servant will justify many, and He will carry their iniquities. Therefore I will give Him the many as a portion, and He will receive the mighty as spoil, because He submitted Himself to death, and was counted among the rebels; yet He bore the sin of many and interceded for the rebels (Isaiah 53).

The Old Testament also prophesies that the Messiah will be rejected by Israel (Isaiah 6:8–10; 53:1–3; 65:1–3). And if you know anything about the crucifixion of Christ, you know that's exactly what happened. So the Bible told the people long before it happened that the Messiah would suffer exactly the way that He did, *"He was despised and rejected by men, a man of suffering who knew what sickness was. He was like someone people turned away from; He was despised, and we didn't value Him. Yet He Himself bore our sicknesses, and He carried our pains; but we in turn regarded Him stricken, struck down by God, and afflicted. But He was pierced because of our transgressions, crushed because of our iniquities; punishment for our peace was on Him, and we are healed by His wounds"* (Isaiah 53:3–5). Jesus was despised, rejected and struck down, and on the cross Jesus was pierced.

Not only that, but Jesus was buried in a rich man's tomb just as was prophesied in Isaiah 53:9. But the most important thing of all foretold about the Messiah in the same verse was His sinlessness, which is confirmed in the New Testament in Hebrews 4:15: *"For we do not have a high priest who is unable to sympathize with our weaknesses, but One who has been tested in every way as we are, yet without sin."*

# THE FINAL SACRIFICE

These appearances and foreshadowings of Jesus seen throughout the Old Testament are evidence of God's continued relationship with His people. But they are only a temporary fix, like the tabernacle that was meant to be taken down and carried to the next location. The presence of the Son of God in the lives of His people before He actually became flesh and lived among us allowed His people the chance to hear from Him through the priests, to get the law through the prophets, and to worship Him through their sacrifices. But even these were not enough to restore the relationship Adam and Eve once had in the garden. **In the end, a Savior was needed, a once-and-for-all deliverer, who would save mankind from sin and make us forever clean, forever acceptable and forever His.** And this Savior was, of course, Jesus Himself, in flesh and blood. It is for Him that the entire Bible was written, and it is for Him that your entire life exists—to make Him the main focus of your life. In the next chapter we will find out more about Jesus as a man and see how He wants to be with you for the rest of your life.

# DISCUSSION QUESTIONS:

*Why does sin require blood to cover it?*

*Why does the Old Testament point forward so many times to the coming of Jesus?*

*What is the purpose of the prophecies of God?*

*What is the difference between a foreshadowing of Jesus and a Christophany?*

*Why do you think God uses so many different foreshadowings of the coming of Christ?*

# OTHER RESOURCES:

*The Gospel Project*

*The Real Messiah: Prophecies Fulfilled*, D. James Kennedy and Jerry Newcombe (2008)

Podcast by Matt Chandler called "Loud and Clear."

http://www.thevillagechurch.net/sermon/loud-and-clear/

# CHAPTER 3
# THE HOLY SPIRIT
# WITH YOU

*When the Spirit of truth comes, He will guide you into all the truth. For He will not speak on His own, but He will speak whatever He hears. He will also declare to you what is to come.* (John 16:13)

In his 1884 work *Flatlands,* author Edwin Abbott wrote about a two-dimensional world filled with people who were essentially drawn on paper. In this land, everything was made up of lines. Their whole world was only length and width. It was like a map. And because of that, the Flatlanders could only see what was right next to them. They couldn't lift up off the page and look, because that would require three dimensions. They could move around their land, but they were limited to their two dimensional space. When a third dimension was explained to them, most refused to accept it. They had no concept of an additional dimension, so they couldn't believe it. But this third dimension gave another being the ability to be right above the Flatlander and yet be unseen by them. Because they didn't live with the dimension of height, they couldn't even see a finger that hovered just above them. Even if that finger were to go right through them, they would have no idea of the being that put it there, only the hole that it left.

A Flatlander might believe the closest person to them is the one drawn next to them, when in fact the one who entered into them is closer than anyone or anything else in their world. Until they open their minds to conceive of a third, even fourth or fifth dimension, they cannot fully grasp the closeness of the being that lives outside their dimension. And so it is with the life of God in the believer. **God lives beyond our limited four dimensions of length, width, height, and time. Because of that, He has the ability to be closer to you than anything or anyone else in the universe,** without you being fully aware of His nature, or even His presence. He does this through His Holy Spirit, who enters into the believer and lives as a continual testament to God's presence in your life.

This idea should help you wrap your brain around the idea of

God's omnipresence, or ability to be everywhere all of the time. How is it that God can be with you always without you seeing Him or realizing that He's right inside the middle of you? The answer is that He is Spirit and lives outside of our limited dimensions. He isn't flesh and blood (John 4:24). Spirit isn't something you can see. Sure, you can sense Him, you can hear Him with your spiritual ears (John 8:47; Romans 11:8), see Him with spiritual eyes (Deut. 29:4; Ephesians 1:18), even taste Him with spiritual taste (Psalm 34:8). But you cannot see or hear God with your physical senses unless He takes on human or angelic form, or speaks through a bush or other entity as He did in the Old Testament. God, in His omnipresence, is unseen but always there. Even in the Old Testament His Spirit was there.

Of the creation of the world we read, *"Now the earth was formless and empty, darkness covered the surface of the watery depths, and the Spirit of God was hovering over the surface of the waters"* (Genesis 1:2). God's Spirit, **the Holy Spirit, was the energy of creation, the doer of the work of God here on the earth.** When God moved on the earth, when He created, when He acted, it was the Holy Spirit acting, moving, and creating. He is the One that made you and gave you life: *"The Spirit of God has made me, and the breath of the Almighty gives me life"* (Job 33:4).

Just like God the Father and Jesus the Son, **the Holy Spirit is eternal** (see Hebrews 9:14), there from the beginning of creation, always existent. **He is one with the Father, just like Jesus. He is in relationship with God, and He is God Himself.** Second Corinthians 3:17 says, *"Now the Lord is the Spirit, and where the Spirit of the Lord is, there is freedom."* The first part of this verse says that God is the Spirit, just as "the Word was God" in John 1. The second part shows the Spirit as an individual, *"the Spirit of the Lord."* As you saw in Genesis 1:2, *"the Spirit of God was hovering"* over the waters. It wasn't the Father hovering over the waters, but *"the Spirit of God."* Isaiah 48:16 confirms this Spirit when the prophet Isaiah speaks and says *"And now the Lord* GOD *has sent me and His Spirit."* God the Father sending. the Son of God and the Spirit going. Three. One.

# From creation until today, and even tomorrow, God's Spirit has been and will be active on the earth.

While God the Son appeared frequently in the Old Testament, the Holy Spirit was also working to teach, to correct, and to direct the people of God. There were many men who not only worshipped God but were controlled by His Spirit. David is one of the most famous examples. First Samuel 16:13 says, *"The Spirit of the LORD took control of David."* The Bible also says that God took His Spirit from Saul. The Holy Spirit was with men like Joseph (Genesis 41:38), Moses (Numbers 11:17), Gideon (Judges 3:10), Samson (Judges 14:6), and more. The prophets also heard from the Spirit before they told the people anything (see Nehemiah 9:30). And in Haggai 2:4–5, God reminds the Israelites that His Spirit would stay with them after they came out of Egypt. *"My Spirit is present among you; don't be afraid"* (v. 5).

**The Holy Spirit, then, is the part of the Trinity who makes a real-time relationship between man and God possible.**

He is the Spirit of God and, because of that, **He knows all of God's thoughts** (see 1 Corinthians 2:10–11). This is crucial, because it is the Holy Spirit who speaks to you, stirs your heart, and tells you what God wants, what He's thinking, and who you are through God's Word. **He is the One who first showed you Jesus.** He is the one who softened your heart and allowed you to see God for the first time, to really see Him. And because of His presence, you were able to understand stuff you couldn't understand before, to see things you didn't used to be able to see. This is called regeneration, the softening of your heart to the things of God, the opening of your eyes. This happened in the Old Testament too, but it was called something different then—"circumcision of the heart." Deuteronomy 30:6 uses this expression when it says, *"The* LORD *your God will circumcise your heart and the hearts of your descendants, and you will love Him with all your heart and all your soul so that you will live."*

Ezekiel calls it getting a "new heart." *"I will give you a new heart and put a new spirit within you; I will remove your heart of stone and give you a heart of flesh. I will place My Spirit within you and cause you to follow My statutes and carefully observe My ordinances. Then you will live in the land that I gave your fathers; you will be My people, and I will be your God"* (Ezekiel 36:26–28). See, without the Holy Spirit, the people were unable to love God, unable to hear from Him, to have relationship with Him. Their hearts were hard, like stone. Moses talks about this earlier when he tells the Israelites who were with him in the desert, "Yet to this day the LORD has not given you a mind to understand, eyes to see, or ears to hear" (Deuteronomy 29:4–5). So even in the Old Testament, people needed the Holy Spirit in order to believe in God and to be accepted by Him.

# HAYLEY'S LITTLE PICTURE

*When I was in high school, I believed in God. I loved Jesus and knew He died on a cross for my sins, but I didn't know the Holy Spirit. I had heard all about God from man, I had sung the songs, prayed the prayer. In fact, I prayed the prayer to ask Jesus into my heart every weekend. I would sit in front of the TV and watch an old televangelist and just sob and cry. I wanted God so badly. But each week I was back to feeling all alone. I tried reading the Bible, but it made no sense. It was literally like reading Greek! I had no sense of God's presence, any sense of His touch or voice. I was all alone. Until one day it all changed, and on that day, all I can say is that the Holy Spirit came to me. I know He came to me because I opened up the Bible and it sprung to life. It was like it was written in invisible ink until that moment, and I was blind to the truth. But all of a sudden, everything I read spoke to my heart. It answered all my questions. It was like the meaning of life in my hands, and that's why I was so ravenous to read it. I was starving; starving to death for truth, for hope, for faith. And there it was, in the blink of an eye. I went from lost to found. And it had nothing to do with me, it was all Him. He revealed Himself to me that day in the form of His Holy Spirit, and life has never been*

*the same. The darkness lifted, the chaos calmed, and the loneliness left me. When the Holy Spirit reveals Himself to you, you will know it because His person and presence confirms the Word of God in our hearts. When Scripture makes sense to you, that's a Holy Spirit moment. When the reading or voicing of Scripture triggers conviction or godly grief in your heart about sin in your life, that's a Holy Spirit moment. And when you feel propelled to repent, lay your shame at the foot of the cross, and then feel freedom from the weight of that sin, that is a Holy Spirit moment! When you are mindful of these moments, you will know Him because He has shown Himself to you!*

# THE HOLY SPIRIT LIFE

Jesus provided the final sacrifice that made peace between you and God. And **the Holy Spirit is your instant access to God the Father.** He is God within you, just as He was God in the lives of the Old Testament believers. And as God's instrument on the earth, He was responsible for the conception of Jesus. As you've probably heard every year at Christmas, *"The birth of Jesus Christ came about this way: After His mother Mary had been engaged to Joseph, it was discovered before they came together that she was pregnant by the Holy Spirit"* (Matthew 1:18). The Spirit gave Jesus to the earth in the long-awaited gift of the Savior, the Messiah, prophesied and foretold for so many years (see Isaiah 7:14). Then, at the end of the Savior's life, the Holy Spirit was given as a deposit of things to come (2 Timothy 1:14). His presence in the world, after Christ's death and resurrection, is better for us than having Christ Himself, still man, walking around the earth. As Jesus says Himself in John 16:7, *"It is for your benefit that I go away, because if I don't go away the Counselor will not come to you. If I go, I will send Him to you."* In this one moment, in the ascension of Christ, God prepares the world for more of the presence of the Spirit than they had ever known. He prepares us to not only have His Spirit descend on us, speak to us, or visit us, but to live with us, to walk with us, to be in us. In this gift of the Spirit you now have access to God 24/7 and forever. In His Spirit your life is changed.

If you've spent any time in church, you've probably heard that **the believer's body is a temple of God.** *"Don't you yourselves know that you are God's sanctuary and that the Spirit of God lives in you?"* (1 Corinthians 3:16). In other words, like the tabernacle of the Old Testament, your body becomes the place where God's Spirit lives. This is a huge concept. And though you can say it, and even believe it, do you know what it really means? How it changes your life? And what it means to your walk with Christ? Knowing that you have God living inside of you should make your life completely different than a person who doesn't have the Spirit in them. It should give you a sense of the Almighty and a desire to want more of Him. And it should give you the things of God—hope, peace, rest, patience, joy, love, and all the other promises of God. But how do those things come into your life? How does the Spirit move? And what is His role once He's a part of your life? The truth is,

**without the Spirit you wouldn't know anything of the true nature of God,**

because the things of God are too deep, too amazing for the human mind to comprehend. That's the condition of the unbelieving mind. It cannot conceive of God and His goodness. But when the mind is invaded by the Holy Spirit, when He turns on the divine light and shows you the words of God found in Scripture and makes them real to you, makes them connect with you, then the truth shines brightly. **The Holy Spirit is the one responsible for revealing Jesus to you**, because, after all, without His divine light you wouldn't be able to grasp the truths of God at all. Jesus explained this revelation to His disciples in the book of Matthew. When Jesus asked Peter who He was, Peter said, *"'You are the Messiah, the Son of the living God!' And Jesus responded, 'Simon son of Jonah, you are blessed because flesh and blood did not reveal this to you, but My Father in heaven'"* (Matthew 16:16–17). See, it wasn't the testimony of man, or even the fact that Peter walked around with, spoke to, or even touched Jesus in the flesh that convinced Him of His deity. It was the Spirit of God Himself who gave this knowledge to Peter from God the Father. Later, Jesus explained the gift of the Holy Spirit: *"When the Spirit of truth comes, He will guide you into all the truth. For He will not speak on His own, but He will speak whatever He hears. He will also declare to you what* *is to come. He will glorify Me, because He will take from what is Mine and declare it to you. Everything the Father has is Mine. This is why I told you that He takes from what is Mine and will declare it to you"* (John 16:13–15). It is the Spirit's job to reveal God to your heart. Now, this doesn't mean that He will give you all kinds of visions or new ideas about Himself. **Beware of thinking that the Spirit is speaking anything that isn't already found in Scripture.** While Muslims and other people groups across the globe are coming to Christ based off of visions and dreams every week, the danger is that if you think that the Spirit is giving you visions, new ideas, new concepts, prophecies, or future stuff that is contrary to and not confirmed in Scripture, you are in danger of listening not to the Spirit but to the false angel of light, Satan, who disguises himself as the Spirit (see 2 Corinthians 11:14). He will try to convince you to listen to him against and over God's own Word.

# HAYLEY'S LITTLE PICTURE

*There was a time when I liked trying to imagine God, to use my imagination to see Him, to talk to Him. I would close my eyes and pray to Him, then allow my mind to imagine what He was doing, saying, allowing Him to take me places. I had visions of what God wanted me to do, what He would do for me. I would imagine people and try to get a vision from God that would tell me which people were my people, and what we would do together. I remember one time when I was in love with a boy, imagining God touching our lives, and in one quick image I saw me with him and our two cute kids, a boy and a girl. And in that instant I was sure I was to marry him. This vision, this "word" from God was a certainty to me. Even though God says we can't even know what we are going to do tomorrow, let alone know our future (James 4:13–16), I was sure I had heard from God. Trouble is, that guy and I broke up a month later, and I was devastated. Not just because I missed him, but because I had missed God. I had heard wrong. I had been mistaken. So what else was I mistaken in believing about Him? It took me awhile to realize that God isn't giving individual revelation to people about His will or their futures, but has given us all that He wanted to give us in His Word. When I realized that, I started to see that everything I heard from God needed to be confirmed by Scripture. If what I believed to be God's will wasn't spelled out in the Bible, it was not His Word at all.*

When the Holy Spirit reveals the truths found in Scripture to your mind, what might have been Greek to you before suddenly makes sense. It's like a light turns on and the Bible becomes a living and powerful Word in your life. You might read something you've read many times before, and suddenly it sinks deeper, makes more sense, says just what you need it to say. This is when the Spirit is speaking to you, showing you the things of God. In these moments, **He is testifying to you about Jesus** (see John 15:26).

You might have heard about Jesus from a friend, a pastor, a parent or a stranger, but unless the Spirit speaks to you at the same time, you will reject the words of man because **without the Spirit you can't know the Son.** *"If anyone does not have the Spirit of Christ, he does not belong to Him"* (Romans 8:9). That means that if you have accepted Jesus, if you trust that His death on the cross was enough to restore your relationship with God, then you have heard from the Holy Spirit Himself. He has revealed truth to you and given you access to the Father. With true revelation, with the deposit of the Spirit into your life, your mind is enlightened and able to see the things of God. That's because the Spirit is the one who links you to the thoughts of God. **He is the presence of God, the voice of God, the power of God in your life.**

And *"When He comes, He will convict the world about sin, righteousness, and judgment"* (John 16:8). See, **His coming into your life is always accompanied with conviction**. That's because as He reveals the things of God to you, your own sinfulness becomes glaring, evident, obvious in its rejection of God's very nature. You cannot come face-to-face with God and not see your own sinfulness. The more you see His beauty, His love, His grace, the more you see your mess, your failure, your selfishness. And

**that's the role of the Holy Spirit; to help you see not only your sinfulness, but your need to be saved from yourself.**

If you look at the life of Christ, at God in the pages of Scripture and think "I believe, I believe," but you don't feel the weight of sin in your life, then the Holy Spirit hasn't revealed God to you. With the presence of the Holy Spirit comes conviction, that guilty feeling that leads you not to depression and isolation, but to a deep desire to confess and to repent, to get the sin out and the life of Christ in. That's why for centuries people have prayed something called "the sinner's prayer." This prayer involves the act of calling yourself what you are, a sinner, of confessing your failure to be perfect, and of thanking God for revealing truth to you through His Holy Spirit. Without the Spirit's promptings, you wouldn't have felt conviction in the first place. He saved you, so the prayer is not some magical incantation, but simply a prayer of surrender, thankfulness, and agreement with the Spirit that you are a sinner saved by grace.

There are nonbelievers who feel guilt, who have a temporal understanding of their own sinfulness, an idea of God's truth, they may have even accepted it as Hayley did before the Spirit came into her life. But without the Spirit they don't have forgiveness for their sins, so their guilt doesn't lead them to salvation but to suffering. **The conviction that comes from the Spirit (good guilt) leads to peace, because the Spirit confirms the saving work of Christ on the cross for the sins of all who believe.** It's like the difference between teaching yourself Chinese and having a native Chinese speaker teaching you Chinese. You can work and work to learn the language, but until you hear it spoken by a native, you will never speak it well, if at all. **The Holy Spirit is your language teacher. He is the native speaker who helps you understand the language of God and teaches you to speak it fluently.** This is described in 1 Corinthians 2:10–11, which says, *"Now God has revealed these things to us by the Spirit, for the Spirit searches everything, even the depths of God. For who among men knows the* *thoughts of a man except the spirit of the man that is in him? In the same way, no one knows the thoughts of God except the Spirit of God."*

# You cannot hear the thoughts of God without the Spirit of God speaking to you.

He is the divine teacher, and His lesson plan is the life of Christ. His job is to teach you all things and remind you of everything that Jesus taught (see John 14:25–26).

# MICHAEL'S LITTLE PICTURE

*It's true, when I was seventeen, I prayed the sinner's prayer. I believed in God, and I accepted Jesus, but then life got busy and I got to work on my future. I was in college, and I wanted to be married more than anything. My goal in life was to find a wife, no matter what it took. I was involved with the college group at a local church and was even told by my college pastor that I should go to seminary and become a pastor. But I had other things in mind, mainly getting hitched. So when the girl I was dating broke up with me because her parents thought I was "going nowhere," instead of me seeing that as God freeing me from entanglements, I ran the opposite way. I had to start working to show any future crush's parents that I had money and a career.*

*Up to that time, I had read the Bible a lot. I had quiet times. But most if not all of that study was centered around what I got from God and how I could have the life that I wanted. It wasn't until I was willing to surrender all my plans and desires to God that the Holy Spirit took hold of Scripture and it made sense to me. At that moment, when I was all alone in a jail cell staring at an old Gideon Bible, the Holy Spirit taught me something about God's Word that I had never grasped before. If I was in Christ, I was a new creation, and by the Holy Spirit the old is dead and the new has come (2 Corinthians 5:17). I'd read that passage before, but it wasn't until this one day that it suddenly made sense to me, and I thank the Holy Spirit for revealing it to me.*

As the Spirit does this, as He leads you to Jesus and teaches you about Jesus, He glorifies Jesus as well. **Everything that the Holy Spirit says or does brings glory to Christ** (see John 16:14). In other words, the Spirit honors Him, praises Him, makes Him the star, gives Him the most important place, makes Him Lord! **If you think, hear, or do anything that doesn't glorify God, you can be sure it isn't from the Holy Spirit.** If there is anything you think you need in your life, that seems to be good for you, if it doesn't glorify Christ, you can be certain it isn't from the Holy Spirit.

# FOCUS ON **PRAISE**

*Most Christians know that praise is a good thing, thanking God for the stuff in your life is a way to honor and glorify Him. But if what you are praising is your own sinful choice, then beware because your sin in no way glorifies God. It's like this: If someone does something to you, like spreads a rumor about you or steals the love of your life, and you get them back, saying "Thank God, they got their just reward!" is not glorifying God but yourself. Getting revenge is a sin, and your sin is never reason for applause, thanks, or praise, no matter how much better you may feel after doing it. The glutton can't say "Thank God for this cake," as he stuffs it in his mouth, because he's thanking God for his sinful self-obsession, which God has no part in. Sin is your response to your flesh, not the Spirit of God.*

The Holy Spirit is called "Counselor" by Jesus in John 14:16. *"And I will ask the Father, and He will give you another Counselor to be with you forever."* **As counselor, the Holy Spirit guides you, helps you figure out life, answers your questions, and advises you what to do. As He shows you who God is and what the Bible says, He gives you help in your walk. He makes God the subject of all your conversations with Him.** Have you ever had a friend like that, someone you could go to with your problems and who would always give you perfect advice, always direct you toward higher things; not toward worry and stress, but hope and peace? Well, that's the job of the Holy Spirit. In every conversation, He advocates for the Father. In other words, His answer will always be heaven sent. He is for you, and He is for God, and so in all your dealings with Him He will point you to Him. If there is ever a time that you sense a pulling away from God, a discontentment, a need for change from faith to fear, then you can be sure that what you're feeling isn't from the Holy Spirit, but from the world, the flesh, or the devil. The Holy Spirit will always turn you toward Christ, not away from Him.

See, the Holy Spirit is on the side of love, of goodness, of all that is perfect. So what He wants in your life is always for your best. Even when life gets out of control, when things look bad, you can be sure that **the Holy Spirit is with you and not only with you, but talking to God about you**. It's called interceding, and He does it for those who belong to God. As you can see in Romans 8:27, "*And he who searches hearts knows what is the mind of the Spirit, because the Spirit intercedes for the saints according to the will of God*" (Romans 8:27 ESV). That means that not only does He hear your prayers, your words, your cries, and counsel your heart, but He speaks to God for you, pleads for you, intercedes for you.

# The Holy Spirit glorifies Christ in you and, as He does that, He teaches you how to become more like Christ.

He reveals truth to you, truth that heals you and grows you in faith, in love, in grace, and in so much more. **The Holy Spirit is essential for wisdom and knowledge**

(1 Corinthians 2:13), **just as He is essential for goodness.** You can try to be good with all your strength. You can follow the letter of the law. You can do everything right and still not be good. That's because goodness doesn't come from you but from God Himself. **When a person is good for goodness sake, they are essentially being good for themselves**, to save themselves, to make themselves look good or to be accepted. This kind of obedience, attempting to be good in your own strength, might work for a while. But eventually it fails, as we saw in the lives of the Old Testament believers. It fails because it has at its heart your own flesh, not the Spirit. To better understand this idea, take a look at Romans 8:6–9, *"For the mind-set of the flesh is death, but the mind-set of the Spirit is life and peace. For the mind-set of the flesh is hostile to God because it does not submit itself to God's law, for it is unable to do so. Those who are in the flesh cannot please God. You, however, are not in the flesh, but in the Spirit, since the Spirit of God lives in you. But if anyone does not have the Spirit of Christ, he does not belong to Him."*

**When your obedience or goodness is self-led or self-glorifying, then it's not goodness at all, but fleshiness.**

And stuff of the flesh rots and putrefies like last week's chicken dinner left in the hot summer sun.

But when the Holy Spirit is the Lord of your life, when He calls the shots, then the fruit—or the outpouring—of your life is fresh, crisp, and nutritious. The best way to see this fruit in your life is to look at the list of the fruit of the Spirit in Galatians 5:22–23: *"But the fruit of the Spirit is love, joy, peace, patience, kindness, goodness, faith, gentleness, self-control. Against such things there is no law."* Each one of these amazing things aren't exclusive to people who have the Holy Spirit in them. There are nonbelievers and even some believers who are not listening to the Spirit that have these in their lives, but there are two reasons why these kinds of fruit are putrid. The first reason is nature. **Someone might have patience because it's a part of their nature.** Their flesh isn't tested with slow or frustrating people. They are naturally patient, like an Olympic ice skater might be naturally gifted with balance and speed. In this case, their patience isn't necessarily a fruit of the Spirit, but of the flesh. It doesn't come from listening to the Spirit over the flesh, but to just doing what the flesh naturally does. This kind of patience, coming from your flesh, doesn't necessarily reveal the presence of the Spirit as much as when a person who has no natural ability to be patient but who struggles with anger and judgment but is supernaturally patient in all things he does. One test of fruit of the Spirit patience for those who are naturally patient is asking yourself this question: "Why am I being patient? Is it to make my life easier by avoiding conflict? Is it so that people will like me and bring me glory?" Of course, we can be self-deceiving in our motives; fooling ourselves over our true intentions, but the following is always true: **the fruit of the Spirit glorifies God because it honors Him, not self.**

And that leads to **the second reason the fruit might show up without the help of the Spirit, and that is out of selfishness**. That sounds harsh, but just listen to us here. Is there is a fruit in your life that you work at in order to get something. For example, you might work at peace so that people don't hate or hurt you? Or you might work at kindness so that others will be kind back to you? **When you do something because of what you can get out of it, that's a fruit of the flesh, not the Spirit.** The Spirit grows fruit in keeping with its role of glorifying God, not man. The Holy Spirit kind of fruit seen in Galatians 5 isn't meant to glorify the person in whom it grows, but the God who grows it. And that happens as the fruit that is grown feeds those around you, not yourself. In other words, like the fruit on a tree isn't for the tree to eat but the people who come to it, so the fruit of the

Spirit glorifies God when it is fed to the people around you, and not to yourself.

So it is with all the gifts of the Spirit; teaching, preaching, etc., they are all meant to increase God, not man. And so like the Old Testament, with its prophets, festivals, and institutions, all are meant to point to God, so is the life filled with the Holy Spirit.

# LIVING IN THE SPIRIT

**Through the Spirit you are first made aware of your sinfulness as you see the perfection of Christ and the mess of your life.**

Once the Spirit turns on the divine light that only He can turn on, you suddenly see things differently, do things differently, live differently. **As He enters you, He gives you an all-access pass to the Father.** Because of that, you are able to pray without ceasing, as Paul says in 1 Thessalonians 5:17, and in that prayer to intercede for others. His Spirit gives you your spiritual senses. He gives you eyes to see and ears to hear, so that you might begin to move in the Spirit, to act with Him always in mind, to live for Him and not yourself. When you have the Holy Spirit living in you, you can cry out to God like a child does for a parent. *"For you did not receive a spirit of slavery to fall back* into fear, but you received the Spirit of adoption, by whom we cry out, 'Abba, Father!'" (Romans 8:15). This crying out to God, calling Him *Abba*, which means daddy, comes from a heart filled with the Holy Spirit. The Holy Spirit gives you the access to God that a child has to a parent, only better; continual, uninterrupted, eternal.

When you focus on the will of God found in the Bible, and you set your mind on the things of the Spirit, the hard things in your life—your trials, drama, and struggles—will fade into the background. The more shallow your depth of field grows, the more brilliant your focus becomes. **God wants you to be in the world, but keep your eyes on Him.** When you do that, you will have the power of God Himself living inside you, and nothing, not one thing, can hurt you or take you away from Him, ever!

> For I am persuaded that not even death or life, angels or rulers, things present or things to come, hostile powers, height or depth, or any other created thing will have the power to separate us from the love of God that is in Christ Jesus our Lord! (Romans 8:38–39)

# DISCUSSION QUESTIONS:

*When you look back, can you remember times in your life when you were sure you were hearing from the Holy Spirit?*

*Did the message to you turn out to be true?*

*If not, then can you see now that they were inconsistent with Scripture or outside of Scripture?*

*Look up Revelation 22:18–19. How might the idea of adding to the prophecies of the Bible relate to our discussion on new inspiration or hearing from God?*

*Take a look at the fruit of the Spirit listed in Galatians 5:22–23 and ask yourself which of them you have. If they are a fruit of the Spirit, a result of the Spirit in you, then why don't you have them all? Knowing that God wants to produce them in your life, what would be your part in growing more fruit?*

# ADDITIONAL RESOURCES:

*The Master's Indwelling* by Andrew Murray (1983)


Podcast by Adrian Rogers: "The Wonderful, Spirit-Filled Life."

http://www.sbts.edu/resources/archives-and-special-speakers/

the-wonderful-spirit-filled-life/

# CHAPTER 4
# YOU WITH GOD

> *If you confess with your mouth, "Jesus is Lord," and believe in your heart that God raised Him from the dead, you will be saved.* (Romans 10:9)

There is a story told of a railroad switchman. His job was to man a lever that moved a section of train track into position for trains to pass. This section of track was over a river. It was kept in a position that allowed boats to pass freely through the water, but when a train was scheduled to come through the area, the track had to be moved by the switchman. Every day he went to his post at exactly the same time. At exactly the right time, he would grab the lever that moved the track into position, allowing the train to pass safely over the river. On one day, however, just as he pulled the lever back and the track began to move into place, he also heard his four-year-old boy calling out, "Daddy, where are you?" The boy had come to visit his father as he had many times before. Only this time he was on the section of the track that would soon be lined up for the train to pass. At that split second, the father had a choice to make. He could either let go of the lever and keep his boy out of the harm of the on-coming train, or he could keep hold of the lever and give the train full of passengers safe passage. His mind raced. Everything in him wanted to save his son and let go of the lever, but he could see the faces of the oblivious passengers and he knew what he had to do. He yelled out, "I'm here son!" and then he dropped his eyes. The train raced past him and into the frail body of his baby boy. The passengers knew nothing of what was given up for them that day. And as the man walked home he hung his head, thinking of how he would explain to his wife what he had done.

This story has been going around since the late 1800s, used to try to give people an inkling of an understanding about what a bitter loss the Son was to the Father who sent Him to die on the cross for all of mankind. And while this story is a powerful one, and can help us in our limited human understanding grasp the depth of the sacrifice of the cross, it doesn't begin to compare to the real story of how God saved us from a death we are as oblivious to as the people on the train. Unlike the switchman, God didn't respond to an emergency. As you saw in the last chapter, He was aware of the sacrifice that would be needed before He even created the world. And the Son, Jesus, wasn't taken by surprise either. He was totally aware that the day on Golgotha was coming. All of creation was in preparation for that one event: the life, death, and resurrection of Jesus. And so it isn't strange that His life is the center point of time. It's where we get BC, "before Christ," and AD—which you might think means "after death," but actually stands for *anno domini,* or "in the year of our Lord." The Old Testament, the New Testament, and the present all revolve around the person of Christ.

The more you understand this, the better you will understand your relationship with God. When you start to see how He has orchestrated the world and His role in it, you can't help but be compelled by the story of Jesus. This center of everything, this reason for hope, this door to the Father, is by far the most important person in your life, whether you know it or not. As long as your life is dominated by feelings of luck or fate, by fear or doubt, you will be a spectator like the kid at the fence, rather than a participant in the big picture of life.

**God gave humanity centuries of life before Christ to prove to us that we couldn't do it on our own, we couldn't be good enough, we couldn't perfect or save ourselves.**

# GUILT

From Adam and Eve, through the end of the Old Testament, mankind has been proving its sinfulness rather than its success. **Every human being that has ever walked this earth has sinned except one, Jesus Himself.** All the rest of us have fallen short. We have chosen self over others, we have feared, hated, worried, gotten revenge, we have been thieves, adulterers, murderers, and thugs. We have shown time and time again our desire to be like God and to rule our own lives and the lives of others. Because of that, God has been unable to live with us like He did in the garden.

In the Old Testament, God gave us an understanding of the path to goodness when He gave us His law. The law showed man what was good and what was evil. **But because of our imperfection, the law made us guilty.** Paul puts it like this in his letter to the Romans, "I would not have known sin if it were not for the law. For example, I would not have known what it is to covet if the law had not said, Do not covet. And sin, seizing an opportunity through the commandment, produced in me coveting of every kind. For apart from the law sin is dead. *Once I was alive apart from the law, but when the commandment came, sin sprang to life and I died. The commandment that was meant for life resulted in death for me. For sin, seizing an opportunity through the commandment, deceived me, and through it killed me. So then, the law is holy, and the commandment is holy and just and good"* (Romans 7:7–12). This all means that without the law there is no sin. But since God taught us the law, taught us what was right and wrong, it gave us the desire to taste and see the difference between right and wrong, to be like God in His understanding, to eat from the tree of knowledge. And when that happened, when sin sprang to life, we died. See, the law points to the path of righteousness, which means it points to life. But when you sin, the law then leads to judgment and death. **Death shows itself in your life in your separation from God.** In that separation, that space between you and God, is all kinds of ugly and deadly stuff—worry, fear, hatred, anger, isolation, bitterness, jealousy, fighting, idolatry, depression—and all the other stuff that pollutes your life. But worst of all is the guilt. **Judgment shows itself in your life as guilt**, in knowing how much you have failed to be who you were meant to be, to love the way you were meant to love, and to do what you were meant to do.

Do you ever feel guilty? Are you ever worried about what your mistakes mean to your relationship with God, to your goodness? Most of the stuff you feel that you call guilt is known as conviction. And like a criminal that sits in court and hears his conviction, the sentence for his crime, your heart convicts and accuses you of sin. When that happens, the harsh reality that you aren't good enough for God sets in. When you realize how sinful and weak you truly are, you get a sense of how powerless you are to change and to fix the mess you've made. In fact, when you mess up, even getting it out of your own memory seems impossible. A lot of times sin can overwhelm you, and your heart, sensing your guilt, can convince you that you need punishment. When that happens, you do things like hate yourself and hurt yourself. Or maybe you just distract or medicate yourself, looking for something that will numb the pain and the memory. You grab a drink, smoke something, play something, chase someone, buy something, whatever you use for turning off the pain of a guilty conscience is your attempt to hide, just the way Adam and Eve hid that day so long ago in the garden.

See, **whether you know it or not, your body was designed to live in perfection.** You were made to be with God, and in His presence to live in purity and peace. So when you mess up, your body and your mind have a negative reaction to it.

# Your heart becomes guilty as it ponders the mess it's gotten itself into, and you realize how unacceptable you are to a perfect God.

As your mistakes, heartaches, and failures add up, your sense of need to be saved from yourself, from this world, grows, and you are faced with two options. You can try to save yourself or you can find someone else to save you.

# FOCUS ON GUILT

*Guilt is uncomfortable. It can make you feel awful and unacceptable. And guilt can lead you to do all kinds of stupid stuff. So it's important to understand when guilt is something that you need to act on (good guilt) and when it's something you need to reject (bad guilt).*

## GOOD GUILT VS. BAD GUILT

**Good guilt is the healthy conviction you feel when you have sinned against God.** It is meant to lead you to action. That action is:

1. To confess and to repent, like it says in 2 Corinthians 7:10: *"The kind of sorrow [guilt] God wants us to experience leads us away from sin and results in salvation. There's no regret for that kind of sorrow. But worldly sorrow [bad guilt], which lacks repentance, results in spiritual death"* (emphasis added, NLT).

2. To accept God's gracious forgiveness (1 John 1:9).

**Bad guilt** [worldly sorrow] is the feeling you get:

a. When **you have not committed a sin** but disappointed someone, been embarrassed, or messed up. In other words, it is shame you feel for something that was not a sin.

b. When **you have confessed and repented but you still feel guilty.**

c. When what you feel **drives you away from God** instead of toward Him.

**Saving yourself means having total self-control and the ability to control the people around you.** Saving yourself also means finding the strength to do what history has proven you are incapable of doing—what needs to be done, rather than what you want to do. Saving yourself means rejecting the part of you that really wants to do what's bad for you. And that means war, civil war, as your good desires and evil desires fight for control of your life. In this battle, you win some and you lose some, and the more you lose the farther back you go. Saving yourself means hard work and failure, and in the end you find out that you are powerless to not only change yourself, but to justify yourself to a holy God.

Then there's the option of finding someone else to save you. Trouble is, everyone else is just as weak as you are. They might promise you salvation, they might give you twelve easy steps to overcome your messed-up life, but they are powerless to stand between you and a God who demands justice when His creation sins against Him. You can't get around or avoid the God who demands death as a penalty for sin. Ultimately, you must answer to Him. And no one can answer to Him for you. Or can they?

# HAYLEY'S LITTLE PICTURE

*When I was in high school, I heard a lot about God's wrath, His anger, and His hatred of sin. It made me look at myself as unsalvageable. I just knew that my messed-up life was too messy for God, and because of that I was going to hell. Sure, I believed in God, I loved Jesus, I even accepted Him as my Savior. But to me that wasn't enough. I needed to be perfect, but I failed over and over again. So I finally just gave up and gave in to sin. I told myself as, "I'm not good enough for God, and if I'm going to hell anyway, I might as well have fun on the way!" And so I did. I started to party and to go a little crazy. It wasn't until a boy I worked with told me about the sticking power of Christ that everything changed for me. "You mean there's nothing I need to do to add to what He did?" "Nope." "You mean He's enough? And I can't lose my salvation whenever I mess up again?" "Yep." Wow, this news changed my life. In fact, these are the exact words that changed my life:* **"If you confess with your mouth, 'Jesus is Lord,' and believe in your heart that God raised Him from the dead, you will be saved. One believes with the heart, resulting in righteousness, and one confesses with the mouth, resulting in salvation"** *(Romans 10:9–10). The idea that there was a way to be cleaned up and acceptable to God blew my mind, and from the second I read these words my life changed forever.*

# WHY DID JESUS COME TO EARTH?

There are a lot of people who think Jesus was just another prophet, a wise man with great teachings. Love one another, turn the other cheek, humble yourself, give, serve, be gentle, kind, and hospitable. While He walked the earth Jesus did say some life-changing things that altered the way people looked at morality for centuries. But if all Jesus was was a wise man with great teachings, then He was a lunatic as well, because He claimed to be God. In John 8:58, He calls Himself "I am," which is what only God can call Himself. And in John 14:6–7 He says that if you know Him you know God. In fact, He goes so far as to say that if you don't believe He is God, then you will die for your sins (see John 8:24).

As you've already seen throughout the Bible, Jesus is more than a prophet, He is actually one with God Himself. So the fact that He came to the earth to live among His people is an amazing fact. Why would God do it? Why not just keep making appearances as the angel of the Lord or symbolizing His presence with the pillar of fire? Why did He submit Himself to becoming a part of the world He had created, like the impossibility of an artist becoming part of His own drawing?

You've probably seen the signs in the stands at football games and on top of church billboards: *"For God so loved the world that he gave his one and only Son, that whoever believes in him shall not perish but have eternal life"* (John 3:16 NIV). This eternal life that Jesus provides is a life that applies to your present as well as your future—in other words, eternity starts now. But heaven is what you probably think of most often when you think of eternal life. And that makes sense, because in less than a hundred years you will move to one of two places forever and ever, and that's a long time.

## Jesus came so that you could spend your forever and ever with God,

not separated from Him, isolated from all that is good, in your own little hell, alone forever (2 Thessalonians 1:9). He came to give you life with Him and the Father, in heaven. And giving you that eternal life He takes away your fear of death (see Hebrews 2:14–15). After all, what is there to fear from leaving this earth and going to heaven?

But eternal life isn't just about heaven and hell, it applies to your right now. Jesus' sacrifice not only saves you for heaven, it saves you from sin. Take a look at one of the most amazing passages in Scripture that proves this point:

For we know that our old self was crucified with him so that the body ruled by sin might be done away with, that we should no longer be slaves to sin—because anyone who has died has been set free from sin. **Now if we died with Christ, we believe that we will also live with him**. For we know that since Christ was raised from the dead, he cannot die again; death no longer has mastery over him. The death he died, he died to sin once for all; but the life he lives, he lives to God.

In the same way, **count yourselves dead to sin but alive to God in Christ Jesus**. Therefore do not let sin reign in your mortal body so that you obey its evil desires. Do not offer any part of yourself to sin as an instrument of wickedness, but rather offer yourselves to God as those who have been brought from death to life; and offer every *part of yourself to him as an instrument of righteousness.* For **sin shall no longer be your master, because you are not under the law, but under grace.** (Romans 6:6–14, emphasis added, NIV)

Did you see it? Did you see your eternal life starting now? **Your eternal life with Christ starts the minute you die with Christ.** In other words, your access to not only salvation, but forgiveness, righteousness, and freedom from the chains of sin starts at the point that you deny yourself (i.e., die with Christ, are crucified) and give Him your worship. When you recognize Him as the Lord of your life instead of yourself you "live with Him." And **as you live with Him, you are dead to sin. In other words, sin isn't your master anymore**. It has no power over you, because you are no longer under the law, but under grace. Under the law your sin led to bondage and death, but under grace, or the kindness of God given to those who accept Christ as the final sacrifice in their lives, you are no longer a slave to sin.

# FOCUS ON SACRIFICE

*The only sacrifice needed for your sins is Jesus. There are no good works you can do to get God to forgive you. Only Jesus can pay for your sins. That's why He came to the earth. That's why He died, and that's why He rose again. You have to understand the importance of His sacrifice in your life!*

I am the good shepherd. The good shepherd lays down his life for the sheep. (John 10:11)

But God proves His own love for us in that while we were still sinners, Christ died for us! (Romans 5:8)

For the Messiah did not enter a sanctuary made with hands (only a model of the true one) but into heaven itself, so that He might now appear in the presence of God for us. He did not do this to offer Himself many times, as the high priest enters the sanctuary yearly with the blood of another. Otherwise, He would have had to suffer many times since the foundation of the world. But now He has appeared one time, at the end of the ages, for the removal of sin by the sacrifice of Himself. And just as it is appointed for people to die once—and after this, judgment—so also the Messiah, having been offered once to bear the sins of many, will appear a second time, not to bear sin, but to bring salvation to those who are waiting for Him. (Hebrews 9:24–28)

By this will of God, we have been sanctified through the offering of the body of Jesus Christ once and for all. (Hebrews 10:10)

But this man, after offering one sacrifice for sins forever, sat down at the right hand of God. (Hebrews 10:12)

**The devil would love to convince you that Jesus isn't enough**, that your sin is so bad that not even His blood could cover it up. But that's a lie, like everything else out of the devil's mouth (John 8:44).

# If your sin is too big, then Christ died for nothing.

If your sin is too big, then He's not the infinite being we think He is, because there is something more powerful than Him, your sin. *"If righteousness could be gained through the law, Christ died for nothing!"* (Galatians 2:21 NIV). But Christ didn't die for nothing, **His death is enough to cover every sin. To think that He can't forgive your sin is to think too highly of yourself** and to listen to the lying mouth of the devil. That's another reason Christ came to the earth—to shut him up, to destroy his work. It says so right in 1 John 3:8: *"The Son of God was revealed for this purpose: to destroy the Devil's works."* And that's exactly what He did when He destroyed the power of death.

No longer does your sin lead to spiritual death, and no longer does it lead to an eternity of separation from God, the worst death of all. The devil tried to ruin it all by leading Adam and Eve into sin, but Jesus redeemed us from the hands of the devil.

So **Jesus came to the earth to give you eternal life, to destroy the works of the devil, and to give you more than you could ever imagine**. *"I have come so that they may have life and have it in abundance,"* He says (John 10:10). If your life is miserable, weak, ineffective, and empty, then you don't have to look any farther. Jesus came to give you more—more of Him, more of love, joy, peace, hope, faith, more and more, and the biggest part of that more is a relationship with God. For centuries God was someone a person could only know about through an intermediary, a priest, or a prophet, but **because Jesus came, you now have access to God yourself**. Jesus shows us this in John 14:23 when He says, *"If anyone loves Me, he will keep My word. My Father will love him, and We will come to him and make Our home with him"* (John 14:23). Wow, now that's relationship, the Father living in you, making His home with you. That's a relationship early believers could only have dreamed of.

# FOCUS ON JESUS

*Why did Jesus come to the earth as a man?*

**To be the final sacrifice**

**To give you eternal life**

**To give you freedom from sin**

**To give you forgiveness**

**To destroy the works of the devil**

**To give you abundant life**

**To teach you about His Grace**

**To be an example of how to live**

# THE GRACE OF GOD

**Jesus came to the earth giving**—life, freedom, forgiveness, and victory. But He also came to give us a better understanding of not only who He is but also who we are. He came to give us the good news about our salvation and to show us what a life of grace looks like (see Mark 1:38). And so He taught. He went from village to village teaching us to live a life of humility, a life of surrender; not to the keeping of the law, but to God the Father. And in one such village He told this story:

> *The kingdom of God is like a king who decided to square accounts with his servants. As he got under way, one servant was brought before him who had run up a debt of a hundred thousand dollars. He couldn't pay up, so the king ordered the man, along with his wife, children, and goods, to be auctioned off at the slave market.*
>
> *The poor wretch threw himself at the king's feet and begged, "Give me a chance and I'll*

*pay it all back." Touched by his plea, the king let him off, erasing the debt. The servant was no sooner out of the room when he came upon one of his fellow servants who owed him ten dollars. He seized him by the throat and demanded, "Pay up. Now!" The poor wretch threw himself down and begged, "Give me a chance and I'll pay it all back." But he wouldn't do it. He had him arrested and put in jail until the debt was paid.*

*When the other servants saw this going on, they were outraged and brought a detailed report to the king. The king summoned the man and said, "You evil servant! I forgave your entire debt when you begged me for mercy. Shouldn't you be compelled to be merciful to your fellow servant who asked for mercy?" The king was furious and put the screws to the man until he paid back his entire debt.* (Paraphrase of Matthew 18:23–34 MSG)

This parable explains in practical terms how the amazingness of God's grace works: *"For you are saved by grace through faith, and this is not from yourselves; it is God's gift— not from works, so that no one can boast"* (Ephesians 2:8–9). We owe Him so much, we've sinned so much against Him. And yet, when we ask He forgives us everything, with no other work necessary on our part. Amazing!

## Jesus teaches us, then, to share this grace with others.

The grace that God gives is for sinners, for imperfect, indebted people, who are powerless to raise the money or blood to pay their debt. His grace is for the impossible, frustrating, mean, and evil people of the world who hurt Him, and even killed Him on that cross. And so He asks the same of us, to forgive (Matthew 6:14–15), to love (Matthew 5:43–48), to help (Luke 12:33–34), and to serve (Matthew 10:44–45) the difficult people of the world.

This was crazy talk to the people of Christ's time who lived with the idea of an eye for an eye and a tooth for a tooth (Exodus 21:24). They lived under the law and, under the law, someone had to pay. But just like God was gracious in giving the life of His Son to save all of us, so we are to imitate Him and give up our rights in order to point the way to Jesus. When we are always fighting, arguing, condemning, and accusing others, or just standing up for our rights, we are living like people in the Old Testament, demanding that the law be met. But Jesus took care of the law, so we are to give up the fight and humble ourselves, die to ourselves, and consider others more important than ourselves (Philippians 2:3). The most vivid example of this is the teaching of Jesus in His Sermon on the Mount. It gives insight into the depths of love that God wants all of us to reach in relating to one another. Take a look at the way the Jesus turns the law upside down and puts love above all.

*You have heard that it was said to our ancestors, Do not murder, and whoever murders will be subject to judgment. But I tell you, **everyone who is angry with his brother will be subject to judgment**. And whoever says to his brother, "Fool!" will be subject to the Sanhedrin. But whoever says, "You moron!" will be subject to hellfire. So if you are offering your gift on the altar, and there you remember that your brother has something against you, leave your gift there in front of the altar. First go and be* reconciled with your brother, and then come and offer your gift. (Matthew 5:21–24)

You have heard that it was said, Do not commit adultery. But I tell you, **everyone who looks at a woman to lust for her has already committed adultery with her in his heart**. (Matthew 5:27–28)

You have heard that it was said, "An eye for an eye and a tooth for a tooth." But I say to you, **Do not resist the one who is evil.** But if anyone slaps you on the right cheek, turn to him the other also. (Matthew 5:38–39 ESV)

You have heard that it was said, Love your neighbor and hate your enemy. But I tell you, **love your enemies and pray for those who persecute you**, so that you may be sons of your Father in heaven. (Matthew 5:43–45)

When Jesus was asked what the greatest commandment was, He said this, *"Love the Lord your God with all your heart, with all your soul, and with all your mind. This is the greatest and most important command. The second is like it: Love your neighbor as yourself. All the Law and the Prophets depend on these two commands"* (Matthew 22:36–40). Jesus summarized all of the law into love; all of the Old Testament summed up into two commands to love God and love our fellow man. And still, we fall short of keeping this law of loving God and loving others, we still fail. But remember that doing everything right, even loving others, is not a path to salvation—Jesus is. Love for God comes only because He loved you first (1 John 4:19), and it's the foundation of all holy action, of all morality and obedience.

**Now, we obey the law, not in order to be loved by Him or saved by Him, but *because* we love Him.**

Jesus changed the way of thinking about God, about ourselves, about our world, and about our place in it.

Jesus came to the earth as God in the body of man. He was 100 percent God and 100 percent man. That means He never quit being God. He was never less than perfect, never less than eternal, never less than He always is. It had to be that way, because in order for us to be saved we needed a perfect sacrifice, one that was spotless, as we saw in the law. And **because Jesus was perfect, He was the perfect once-and-for-all sacrifice**. But He was still 100 percent man as well. That means that He lived through the same kinds of temptations that you live through every day. He had to eat and sleep. **He allowed Himself to become man so that we could know that He truly gets us** (Hebrews 4:14–15), that He isn't a distant God who only creates and watches from above. He is a God who has walked in your shoes and understands your pain. **He became a man so that He could be an example of how you should live.** And that should give you hope because it means that if He says you can do something, you can do it. He lived the commands of God and didn't fail on any point. He lived through great pain and strain and didn't give into fear or doubt. He lived the kind of life that you too can live, if you are only willing to let Him in—not just visit, but to take up residence and live in you, guiding you and teaching you, helping you and comforting you.

**Jesus fulfilled all of the prophecies about Himself.** He was the perfect image of the foreshadowing we saw throughout the Old Testament. He is God, the Creator of all, there from before the beginning of time, here for thirty-three years, and still with you through His Holy Spirit. While Jesus walked the earth He lived alongside men and women. He interacted with them, He loved them, and He called them friends. And He will do the same with you every day of your life if you only believe that He is who He says He is and that He is all you need both in heaven and here on the earth. If your life hasn't been what you dreamed it could be, if you are tired of the sin that controls you, then consider what you've seen in the life of Christ to be the only missing link.

# HAYLEY'S LITTLE PICTURE

*Most of my life I felt like I was living in a glass ball, living in the world, but watching it from a distance—not able to fully relate, to find my way, to connect, to truly live. This feeling of something being wrong haunted me for years. It threatened me, my joy, my peace, my sanity. It made me question why? And it made me want to end it a time or two. But once I started to see that this life isn't so much about me and my little world but about Him and His big hand in this world, the glass started to break. Once I saw the big picture of God's plan not only for me but for the entire world I was set free. The lights went on, the shade was lifted, and I was able to truly live in the world, to connect with the creation, and to find a purpose far greater than I had ever dreamed. After giving up my pursuit of freedom and joy through fame, I turned my life over to God and His will and, just as He had promised, He gave me more than I ever dreamed possible. My story isn't unique. It happens to all believers who turn their eyes away from themselves and onto Jesus, and it can happen to you today. Even if you are already a Christian, perhaps the Lord is convicting you of more sin and challenging you to surrender to Him in everything—that He might be more important than you (Mark 8:34; Ephesians 4:22–24).*

# DISCUSSION QUESTIONS:

*Read:*

John 6:40

Romans 10:9

1 Timothy 1:15

1 John 1:9

Think about your feelings of guilt. If it is a sin against God, put it in the good column. If it isn't a sin but embarrassment, failure, or disappointment, put it in the bad column.

Now, if you agree that God is right in calling the good column sin, then confess your sin and agree not to do it anymore. Then thank Him for His forgiveness. If you have any guilt in the bad column, then confess to God that you were making something or someone more important than He. Confess your failure to trust Him, to worship Him, to love Him. Confess that it isn't sin, or that you let your fear of not being perfect get between you and God. Just consider both columns as a chance to confess where you were failing to make God Lord of your life, then let them both go.

*"From then on Jesus began to preach, 'Repent, because the kingdom of heaven has come near!'"* (Matthew 4:17). What is repentance? Are there some habits, some things that you are doing that God wants you to change? Promise repentance today.

# OTHER RESOURCES:

The following are all Public Domain, Google them:

*The Pursuit of God* by A. W. Tozer

*Why Do You Not Believe?* by Andrew Murray

*How to Know if You are a Real Christian* by Jonathan Edwards

Podcast by David Platt: "The Urgency of Eternity."

http://www.radical.net/media/series/view/176/the-urgency-of-eternity?filter=book&book=37

# CHAPTER 5
# GOD LEADING YOU

*Therefore, whether you eat or drink, or whatever you do, do everything for God's glory.* (1 Corinthians 10:31)

One day a King and Queen in a land far, far away were bringing their new little prince home from the royal hospital. On the same day, a poor pauper's cart carried a man and his wife bringing home their poor baby from the midwife's house. As they passed one another, a wheel fell off the carriage and it crashed into the pauper's cart. The two families were thrown to the ground and in the chaos the Queen picked up the pauper's baby. So the prince went home to be raised by the poor family.

As the baby grew into a boy, he was often out in the streets begging for food. Little did he know that the streets he begged on belonged to him because they belonged to his real father. Every day as he walked he would stop at the gates of the palace and look longingly inside, sensing that he was meant to live there, but believing that to be a fantasy. And each day he would walk away thinking that he wasn't worthy to have such a life, completely unaware that he was born into royalty and meant to live the life of a prince. And so he lived his whole life with a sense of lacking. He resented his life. He resented the prince and the king. And he never found the truth that would set him free.

When you see the truth, it really does set you free (John 8:32). And the truth is that you were meant to live an abundant life (John 10:10), not a life of want, darkness, fear, worry, doubt, or hate.

# You were meant to be free.

That freedom doesn't come from begging in the streets and dreaming of life within the palace gates as the pauper, but it comes from living with the King. This living is the act of abiding with Him every day of your life. And it doesn't require an influx of cash or a new address, but a mindfulness of the Spirit Himself living within the gates of your heart. When Jesus was leaving the earth He told His disciples, **"Remember, I am with you always, to the end of the age"** (Matthew 28:20). And He's telling you that today. He is always with you. You don't need to beg Him for His presence, just recognize it. You don't need to look for salvation anywhere but in His eyes. And when you recognize your inheritance, you see that you are a child of the King an amazing thing happens: you learn to abide in Him, to live knowing that you are His. When you do that, your life takes on a new form, a new meaning, and in that transformation comes all that you need for a holy and beautiful life. As it says in 2 Peter 1:3, *"His divine power has given us everything required for life and godliness through the knowledge of Him who called us by His own glory and goodness."*

As a child of the King, you were meant to live a life of godliness, of goodness. But sometimes, that isn't how it all comes out, is it? Sometimes it's a big ol' mess, and the only stuff you seem to be able to do is bad, destructive, and just plain stupid. Sure you want to do good, but for some reason you feel powerless. We can say that with certainty, because there is no perfect person but Christ. And since you aren't Him, you are powerless to be good, let alone godly. That's why it's good news that Jesus never leaves you, that He gives you His Holy Spirit to guide you and to help you. Left to your own devices, you will ultimately mess everything up, just like every other person on the planet. But being a child of God changes things. As Paul put it in Ephesians 2:10, *"For we are His creation, created in Christ Jesus for good works, which God prepared ahead of time so that we should walk in them."* God doesn't save you so that you can live a bad or miserable life. He doesn't save you so that you can sit back and enjoy the ride, or dive in and go after all the happiness you can get your greedy little hands on. No, when God saves you, He saves you for the most important thing in the world—Himself. You live to glorify Him, but He shares with you all that He is, all His goodness, grace, love, kindness, and on and on.

# BELIEF ISN'T WORSHIP

Many believe in God, even the demons do, but God only shares Himself with those who give up their lives for Him. You might have believed in God all your life. Faith might run in your family, but that's not the same thing as having a relationship with Him. And it's not the same thing as salvation.

**Belief isn't the same as worship.**

In James 2:19 it says, "*You believe that God is one; you do well. The demons also believe—and they shudder.*" This means that even if you are certain that God is who He says He is, that's not all there is to being a child of God. Saving faith goes beyond belief to surrender. The child of God surrenders Himself to the Father. In other words, He gives up his own rights, desires, hopes, and dreams, and lays them at the feet of God. And in return, He asks for nothing but to spend eternity with Him, loving Him forever. This perfect life, this life in relationship with God, is the foundation of not only your salvation, but of your hope, your peace, and your joy. It's the source of your love, your self-control, your faithfulness. Without this kind of faith that penetrates your life so deeply that it changes your thoughts about God and your thoughts about yourself, as well as your actions, your faith will not save you (see James 2:20–24).

This surrender starts the moment the Holy Spirit reveals your sinfulness to you. When He shows you the depths of your filth, He begins to teach you the act of surrender. The confession of your sinfulness fuels the knowledge of His righteousness. In other words, if you see no sin in your life then you cannot truly see the righteousness of God. But when you see your weakness and sin you also see His power and beauty, and you want less of you and more of Him. And out of this comes your worship.

> **Worship involves the act of surrender. You worship whatever you give your life to.**

So it could be said that if you give your life to music, then, in effect, you worship music. That's because you serve music, you do all you can for music, you think about music all day, you give music credit for your joy, your life, your entertainment, etc. You adore music. So you give it all of the glory. You spend your energy evangelizing your favorite band or artist. You want more of them. You find others to fellowship with and share your excitement with. Ultimately, you end up controlled more by the music than by the God who gave it to you. So in this little example of how surrender happens in the stuff of this world, you can see an analogy of surrender to the Holy Spirit.

# APPRECIATION

**When you make Jesus the Lord of your life you surrender your time, energy, and even thoughts to Him.** The Holy Spirit compels you to want to spend time with Him. Just like you might spend time with your favorite movie star, if you could ever meet them, you want to spend time with your God whom you have met. In that time with Him you do what others who surrender their lives do, you appreciate Him. You thank Him for all He is and all He does. **Worship requires appreciation** and is essential in the life of faith, as you can see throughout the book of Psalms. Like in this psalm of thanks written by King David: *"You turned my lament into dancing; You removed my sackcloth and clothed me with gladness, so that I can sing to You and not be silent. LORD my God, I will praise You forever"* (Psalm 30:11–12). It is impossible not to be thankful when you see all that God has done. Surrender always has a part in thanksgiving.

# ADORATION

**Surrender also requires adoration.** This isn't an "I do this because I have to" kind of thing, but an "I'm amazed how much you give and how much I don't deserve this" kind of thing. It's like when you get an extravagant gift and it's not even your birthday. Or when a friend goes out of their way to be there for you. You don't even think about food or sleep because their love for you causes you to love and adore them in return. This is adoration, and it's exactly what happens when you come face to face with the God of the Bible. **As His Holy Spirit shows you who He is your jaw drops and your heart**

**leaps and you adore Him.** The psalms are full of man's adoration for God. In Psalm 103 David just can't contain his praise: *"My soul, praise Yahweh, and all that is within me, praise His holy name. My soul, praise the* LORD, *and do not forget all His benefits. He forgives all your sin; He heals all your diseases. He redeems your life from the Pit; He crowns you with faithful love and compassion. He satisfies you with goodness; your youth is renewed like the eagle"* (vv. 1–5). Adoration comes a lot in the form of music. We call the singing part of church "worship," because the songs we sing adore Him. But worship isn't just about music. You can also just speak your adoration of Him. All that matters is that you open up your mouth and voice your love and devotion and your praise for who He is and what He has done.

Now, let's remember that God doesn't need your adoration. He's not some megalomaniac looking for ways to feel good about Himself. No, the adoration you give Him is organic. It must come out of you because of the mere amazingness of His being. It's like when you see an incredible snow-covered mountain up close and you smell the fresh air and hear the clear chirping of the birds, you can't help but breathe deep. Your heart fills with awe and you adore what you see before. **Adoration is the organic outpouring of a heart that comes into contact with**

**perfection.** When the Holy Spirit reveals God to your heart it must worship, it must adore with all of its strength. Adoration comes naturally to a child of the King.

# AFFECTION

Affection is also natural in the life of faith. There are some families who are cold. Some never say "I love you," don't talk much with one another, hold one another, or spend time together. But there are many others who say "I love you" every day. These families have real affection for one another. They like each other and so they share their lives with one another. Affection is the natural outpouring of a love relationship, and so it's a natural part of your relationship with God. But since God is a Spirit, how do you show Him affection? Through hugging a tree? Not unless you're from Oregon like us! Ha! No, you show God affection by spending time with Him, talking with Him, listening to Him, reading His Word, and sharing your life with Him.

There are a lot of people who are super busy and don't get to see much of the people they love, and so they have built their lives around the importance of "quality" over "quantity" when it comes to time. These people make the assumption that when you love someone it's better to spend a little good time with them than a ton of all kinds of time. And while this might be born out of necessity here on the earth, in the heavenly realm that just isn't the case. In fact, the children of God will one day spend every single second of eternity with God. There will be no such thing as quality time any more. And while that's our future hope, it is also our present condition. God is omnipresent, living inside of you, He is not with you for just a few minutes of quality time a day. He is there all day long. That means that He sees all you do and hears all you say and all you think. He is not content to be a silent viewer, watching you go about your life, ignored and tucked neatly into your heart. No, He wants to be in continual conversation with you, informing your every thought, your every move, and your every feeling.

Prayer isn't just something you do fifteen minutes a day and call it done. No, according to Scripture it's much, much more. In 1 Thessalonians 5:17, when Paul says to "Pray without ceasing," He isn't exaggerating. He is showing you that God is always present and always wants you to remember that. As God says in Joshua 1:9, ***"Do not be afraid or discouraged, for the LORD your God is with you wherever you go."*** This presence doesn't just mean that you know He is with you, but that you are mindful of His thoughts in all that you do and think. This is another part of surrender. It's so easy for people to say they are Christians and then to only think about God once a week on Sunday. But that is the mark of a cold family, not of a loving one. The family of God is first of all loving. Because of that, we don't just think about God or talk to Him only on Sundays, but without ceasing, every single day. Sure there will be times when your mind is on other things. There will be hours when you don't whisper a prayer because you have a calculation to make or a problem to solve, but the child of God cannot go anywhere or do anything that would completely sever the ability to return to God in prayer and ask for forgiveness.

# GLORIFICATION

Your surrender isn't a one-time thing. It's a daily looking away from yourself and toward God. It's a daily confession of sin, and a turn of repentance. It's a minute-by-minute need for God and the desire to have His fingerprints all over your life. When you take a look at the Bible and see how Jesus lived to glorify God, every second of every day, and you see that He never did anything that would keep Him from praying at the same time. You also see how the Holy Spirit came to the earth to glorify God, to change the conversation back to Him over and over again, and you see a glimpse of your own purpose on the earth. As it says in many ancient explanations of our faith, the chief end, or purpose of man, is to glorify God. Just like Christ lived to point others to the Father, so you live to do the same. So when you are not doing that, when you get lost in the minutia of the daily grind, you lose sight of your purpose. And when you lose sight of your purpose your life pays the price in stress, worry, fear, doubt, and darkness.

But when you keep your eyes on the Father, when you prefer His kingdom and His will over your own, you live life the way you were made to live it. When you live to glorify God what happens to you become irrelevant, and in the process you become surprisingly resilient in suffering, having given up your needs to His will. Knowing His will is always done sets you free from the need to fix things, to complain about things, or to control things. Resting in the peace that His will is always done allows you to endure trials with the knowledge that it produces endurance in you. In the act of glorifying God you find the glory of God within you, pouring out into your life and the lives of those around you. When that happens you are content even when others outshine you (see Philippians 1:15). You fearlessly confess your sins, wanting the purity of Christ over the appearance of perfection (see James 5:16). You believe, you don't doubt (see Romans 4:20–22). And you determine that whatever major life choices you make you will make for His glory and not your own.

That means that the decision about what job you will do, who you will marry, where you will live are all based on what, who, and where gives God the most glory.

# MICHAEL'S LITTLE PICTURE

*I had already decided to give my life and my wife over to God by the time I started dating Hayley. That meant I was looking for someone who would amplify my ministry or service to Him. And that's why I picked Hayley. She made me a better man for God. She didn't encourage my sin, but encouraged me to holiness. She wasn't resistant to giving up her life for God, she was living it. And so her life and mine, put together into one, became the most glorifying relationship I had. When I realized this, I knew without a doubt that she was the one for me. Even though we aren't perfect together—we had a lot of arguments, lived through a lot of difficulties understanding each other—I still know for sure that she is the best one for me because in marriage with her I am able to glorify God more than I did when I was single. And that is the purpose of marriage, work, or anything else in the life of faith—to glorify God more!*

# DISCIPLESHIP MAKING

**The moment the Holy Spirit showed you who Christ truly is, you became His disciple.**

Like the disciples who walked the earth with Him, when God reveals Christ to you, you give up everything else and follow Him. And that's what the modern disciple does, follows Jesus wherever He leads. Discipleship is important to Jesus, so important in fact, that His last words before His ascension into heaven were, *"All authority has been given to Me in heaven and on earth. Go, therefore, and make disciples of all nations, baptizing them in the name of the Father and of the Son and of the Holy Spirit, teaching them to observe everything I have commanded you. And remember, **I am with you always, to the end of the age"*** (Matthew 28:18–20). Jesus wants us to make disciples.

A lot of people look at this Great Commission as a command to tell as many people as you can the gospel message, the good news of Jesus. And while it is true that you are to tell the world about Him, this passage isn't just about making converts but disciples. For the most part, a convert refers to a person at the moment in time when they first believe. And while we are all converts at one point in our lives, we must move from being converts to disciples. Now in order for someone to be converted, or saved, they must hear about Jesus. As it says in Romans 10:14, *"But how can they call on Him they have not believed in? And how can they believe without hearing about Him? And how can they hear without a preacher?"* And telling them has been a big topic of discussion among believers for centuries. There are really three different ways people go about making disciples.

**We call the first one the cold conversations. This is the conversation about God that starts with a stranger.** People who are drawn to this method might be seen using a megaphone on a street corner, or handing out tracts downtown or at big attractions or special events. Ray Comfort and Kirk Cameron have a very direct and compelling way of starting cold conversations with people that leads them to really start thinking about God and their eternal destiny. It's called *The Way of the Master,* and it's a helpful tool to consider using in this kind of witnessing.

**The second we will call foreign conversations.** For centuries, missionaries have felt the call to go to foreign lands and have conversations with indigenous people who might never have heard about Jesus if the missionaries hadn't come to live among them. The beginning of the conversation for missionaries might just be serving people through projects like building schools, digging wells, or treating the sick. In long-term mission situations believers enter into foreign cultures, learn their ways, make themselves a part of the community, and build relationships. But many more people go on short-term mission trips, where they go into a culture for a fairly short period of time to serve and do what they can while they're there. They may help out physically with the people, or even share the gospel with them, but they are in and out.

Both the cold conversation and the foreign conversation aren't for everyone. There are far more people who don't feel equipped either in personality or gifting for either of these forms of evangelism. But the third style is not only suitable for everyone, but commanded repeatedly in Scripture (see Matthew 5:14–16; Luke 6:40; John 15:8; John 13:35; 1 Peter 2:9–10; Titus 2:1–8). We will call these **daily conversations**. This is a style of discipleship that happens on a day-to-day basis wherever you are. When you live to glorify God you find that God puts people around you whom He wants you to serve. These might be people who are familiar strangers, or they might be close friends, but they are people who need more of Jesus. Believers or nonbelievers, either way, making disciples includes encouraging them, helping them, reminding them, and even sometimes getting on them about their sin. But it is always about glorifying God, not yourself, and pointing others to Him.

This style is different from the other two because there are other things going on in the relationship besides you coming to preach the gospel. For example, you might have a teacher or a boss with authority over you, or even a parent that isn't a believer. You can't walk around handing them tracts or building them wells. And bringing a bullhorn into McDonald's during your shift would most likely get you fired. It might be someone who sits next to you on the bus every day, and you don't see them more than five minutes at a time, so discipleship becomes a slow and extended process. It's in this area of life, the day-in and day-out places, where most of us are meant to share our faith. In these daily interactions, you can share Jesus with people by simply feeding them the fruit of His Spirit, by being His hands and feet, and by serving them out of love for them rather than love for self. Build relationships with them, find out their fears, their worries, their needs, and care enough to help them. When people see this fruit of the Spirit in your life they see a glimpse of God. As we said earlier, the fruit in your life that comes, supernaturally from the Spirit within you not from your own will power, isn't meant to feed you and make you happy. It's meant to feed those around you. When hard times hit and those around you see your peace and faith, they will know there is something stronger than self-control going on. When others hurt you and you don't retaliate but live in a love that forgives all things, trusts all things, and hopes all things, they will see the hand of God entering their lives. You are meant to shine the light of truth on the lives of those around you and to be a beacon that points upward, not with harsh words that preach at your friends and acquaintances, but with loving and grace-filled actions that reveal the Spirit of God in you.

Most people tend to believe people who love them and invest in them more than strangers who pop in and pop out with a quick message. Though that has worked many times, and continues to be a way the Holy Spirit can touch a person's life, many more people have come to know Jesus while living in a relationship with another person. In fact, in many countries people won't even listen to your views on God until they know you quite well and you have proven yourself through actions rather than words.

Some missionary acquaintances of ours interviewed locals in a nation that is hostile to Christianity and found out some interesting things. But the biggest thing they found might surprise you. They discovered that many missionaries had moved to the land to serve and witness to the life of Christ, and all had failed but one. When they asked the people why this man was such a successful witness, they said, "Because he needed us." The people trusted him not because he had it all together and preached his perfect life to them, but because he lived with them, cared for them, and he also let them care for him. When a family member died stateside the man didn't have enough money to fly home for the funeral. The people heard about it and got the money together for him. He accepted their generous gift. Rather than refusing on the grounds that he was meant to serve them, he allowed them to care for him, thus establishing a friendship. Rather than having a superior attitude, in love, he let them love him back, and that changed their lives.

# THREE KINDS OF FRIENDSHIPS

**Discipleship takes place in a loving relationship with another human being.** It is a process, not a point in time. It is walking with another, helping them, loving them, and encouraging them. So when God tells you to go and make disciples that isn't just reserved for the foreign missionary or the sidewalk preacher, it's for you, today, in relationship with all the people around you.

**We all have three different kinds of relationships in our lives.** Each one involves a level of discipleship, because in every relationship we are to be making more of Jesus, either by telling others about Him or by learning more about Him from others. You can think of your relationships like a ladder. You are in the middle of the ladder. **Above you are people more mature in their faith than you are. These are the people who disciple you.** They are the people you go to when you are hurting, when you are worried, or need answers. These people encourage your faith, they pray for you, and they hear your confessions, as we saw in James 5:16. They are the "righteous" people.

Then there are people who are below you on the ladder. These **people are less spiritual than you are. And these are the people you are meant to disciple**. Since they are less mature in their faith than you are, these people cannot be your best friends. They can't be the people you go to for counsel, for prayer, for help, because they are not equipped spiritually to lead you toward Christ. That's your role in their lives. In fact, in this category of disciples there are also nonbelievers.

### A disciple isn't always a believer.

The Bible talks about Jesus' disciples in a broad sense as those who followed Him around. We know that because some of them quit following Him when they heard the hard things He was saying (John 6:60–64).

You can disciple someone who hasn't yet come to a saving knowledge of Jesus, but you must beware. A lot of times people use this as an excuse to missionary date, to date a nonbeliever in order to convert him or her. But discipling the opposite sex is never a good idea, especially when they are nonbelievers. God has made it clear that He doesn't want believers to be married to nonbelievers (see 2 Corinthians 6:14). And whether you admit it or not, dating often leads to marriage. If your nonbelieving friend is the same sex, then your job as a believer is to disciple them, not to turn to them for your spiritual or emotional needs. Always be the more spiritually mature one, and encourage them to trust Jesus.

Now, **the people who are on the same spiritual rung as you, those are the ones who can be your best friends.** They know they are at the same spiritual place as you are, so they won't pull you down a rung or lead you astray. They can witness your life and point you toward God. They might not have all the answers, as someone more mature than you may, but at least they aren't weaker and more needy, and so unequipped to guide and pray for you.

**In every relationship there is room for discipleship.** In some you will be the disciple and in others they will be. Either way, making disciples is a lifelong process. It's something you will always be doing if your life is consumed with bringing glory to God. Like adoration that flows naturally from your love for Him, so discipleship should flow from your love for Him.

# SALVATION THROUGH JESUS, NOT YOU

In all relationships it is important to remember that it isn't through your clever or well-placed words that people are saved, but through the Holy Spirit Himself (Matthew 10:20). Your gospel discussions with the people around you all flow out of God's love for them through you. The saving work is up to Him, you cannot change or save anyone. You have to trust that the Holy Spirit is in control of the process of salvation (John 6:44). After all, not even Jesus converted everyone. There were many who walked away from Him, doubted Him, and rejected Him. It wasn't because Jesus wasn't convincing enough or didn't have the power to convince, but because of God's will. As it says of the believer in John 15:16, *"You did not choose Me, but I chose you."* In fact John the Baptist said, *"No one can receive a single thing unless it's given to him from heaven"* (John 3:27). And Paul echoed that in his letter to the Romans: *"So then, He shows mercy to those He wants to, and He hardens those He wants to harden"* (9:18). Making disciples isn't about the hard work that you do, but the work of the Holy Spirit in their lives.

When you look at the big picture of the Bible, you see that none of it is about how hard you work, but all of it is about God and His mighty work.

## The Bible is never meant to be a to-do list

that you follow through self-discipline and struggle. It is meant to be a living record of the love of God in your life and the answer to your search for purpose in this world. When you look at the gospel thread that runs through the entirety of Scripture, when you realize Jesus is the focus of all the Bible, you can see beyond a shadow of a doubt that He is the star. Not only the star, but the main focus of all of life. And as long as your focus is anything other than Jesus your life will be a big blur and your purpose will not be clear. Take what the Holy Spirit has revealed to you as you've gone through this study and allow it to direct every ounce of your thoughts, energy, and life upward. Focus on the Father, the Son, and the Holy Spirit. See their hand on every moment of your life, knowing that these words in Lamentations are true: *"Who is there who speaks and it happens, unless the Lord has ordained it? Do not both adversity and good come from the mouth of the Most High?"* (3:37–38). The whole of Scripture proves this to be true. Nothing happens in heaven or on the earth that takes God by surprise, both the good and the bad. And since He is infinite in His goodness, love, and power, then He is working everything (even bad things) for the best.

Finally,

# wherever you put your focus you put your faith.

If you put your faith in being good, in pleasing your parents, your bosses, or your friends, then your faith rests in your ability to be good or to please. Faith is about focus. When you take a look at your life, where is your focus? If you can't say that Jesus has been the main focus of your life then today should be a really good day, because today can be the first day of a deeper faith in Christ. The entire focus of the Bible is God; who He is and the relationship between God and man, especially the lengths to which God would go for that relationship. And all of it hinges on the life, death, and resurrection of Jesus. You can't read the Bible the same anymore, not after seeing Him in every page and seeing that it all points to His glory. And you can't look at yourself the same anymore either. Just like the Holy Spirit lives to glorify God, so you live to glorify Him as well, *"For you were bought at a price. Therefore glorify God in your body"* (1 Corinthians 6:20). When you understand and embrace this new perspective, by God's grace, you've now got *The Big Picture.* You'll never look at God, yourself, or your life the same!

# ABOUT THE AUTHORS

Hayley and Michael DiMarco are the best-selling authors of almost forty books, including their number-one best sellers *God Girl, God Guy, Devotions for the God Girl,* and *Devotions for the God Guy.* Before selling well over a million books, Hayley spent the early part of her career working for a little shoe company called Nike in Portland, Oregon, and for Thomas Nelson Publishers in Nashville, Tennessee. Michael has worked in broadcasting, coached college volleyball, worked at a major Bible software company, and is currently serving as Minister for Young Adults and Leadership Development at their local church. Together, they run a publishing company called Hungry Planet. You can find out more about Hungry Planet at www.hungryplanet.net.

Follow Hayley at:

godgirl.com

facebook.com/hayley.dimarco

twitter.com/hayleydimarco

Follow Michael at:

godguy.com

facebook.com/michael.dimarco

twitter.com/dimarco